THE LIFE AND POETRY OF JAMES THOMSON

206

James Thomson.

A. Evershed. 1883.

# THE LIFE AND POETRY OF JAMES THOMSON
## (*B. V.*)

BY J. EDWARD MEEKER, M.A.

*"Sunt lacrymae rerum,
et mentem mortalia tangunt"*

NEW HAVEN: YALE UNIVERSITY PRESS
LONDON: HUMPHREY MILFORD
OXFORD UNIVERSITY PRESS
MDCCCCXVII

TO
GEN. HENRY A. BISHOP
THIS BOOK IS AFFECTIONATELY DEDICATED
BY THE AUTHOR

# FOREWORD

Thomson's curious pen name "B. V." is derived from the initials of Bysshe (the middle name of his beloved Shelley), and of Vanolis (an anagram upon the German "Novalis"). It was as "B. V." rather than as James Thomson that the poet was known to his own generation of readers. The present generation, however, has exhibited more curiosity if not more sympathy toward the personality of Thomson. So close a connection exists between the poet's life and his poems, that the reader can scarcely comprehend the latter while in ignorance concerning the former. This has been especially true since Mr. Salt's lengthy biography became almost unobtainable. The present volume is novel chiefly in the fact that more than the few previous sketches of Thomson's life it attempts a close correlation of "B. V.'s" life and his poems.

The author must confess to having made free with Mr. Salt's book, as well as Mr. Dobell's valuable Memoir, and much contemporary periodical criticism. The over-curious reader may even detect passages where the present author has despaired of improving upon the phrases of his predecessors, but has forgotten always to designate them by scrupulous quotation marks. The author at any rate cheerfully admits this clerical fallibility, and would not churlishly grudge any higher student of English his lonely glee in discovering such cases.

The author wishes to acknowledge his indebtedness in the preparation of the present volume to Mr. E. Byrne Hackett, formerly director of Yale University Press, for invaluable suggestions and encouragement; and to Professors C. M. Lewis and C. B. Tinker of Yale, as well as to Messrs. E. T. Webb and W. H. Lowenhaupt and the printers, for numerous criticisms and corrections upon the MS.

J. E. M.

New Haven, Conn.
February 1, 1917.

# TABLE OF CONTENTS

Note:—The frontispiece portrait of James Thomson is after an etching made by A. Evershed in 1889, which appears in Dobell's edition of THE POETICAL WORKS, London, 1895.

# CHAPTER I

## THE REPUTATION OF JAMES THOMSON

JAMES THOMSON died in 1882, after a life which he himself had characterized as "a long defeat." In many details his sorrowful career resembles that of our American poet, Poe. Both poets were orphaned children, and later endured the drudgery of an uncongenial profession. Both survived the woman whom they loved, and finding that her image persisted in their thoughts, preserved her in their poems. Both underwent the privations and poverty of an apparently unsuccessful literary life, at length resorted to stimulants as a desperate escape from their memory, and finally found death in a strange hospital, apart from all their friends. Yet Poe had not long to wait for even a Continental reputation, while James Thomson is still a misunderstood and half-forgotten poet. Whatever Thomson's virtues are as a poet, and they grow more and more impressive on study, his failure to gain popularity is hardly without the malice of fate. For over twenty years, his poems appeared in the minor English magazines, such as the *London*

*Investigator,* the *National Reformer, Tait's Magazine* or *Cope's Tobacco Plant,* and always under the pen-name of "B. V." Although his poetry brought him the friendship of George Meredith, P. B. Marston, the Rossettis, Froude, Kingsley, Saintsbury, and even George Eliot, yet the public was almost unaware of his existence. No attempt was made to collect any of his poems until 1880, when Bertram Dobell published "The City of Dreadful Night, and Other Poems." Encouraged by the sale of this book, which reached its second edition in 1888 and its first American edition in 1892, Dobell published another volume, "Vane's Story and Other Poems," in 1881, without, however, the success of his first venture. In the same year an attempt by Dobell to popularize Thomson's best prose by a collection entitled, "Essays and Phantasies," was rewarded by popular apathy and critical hostility. Thomson's stylistic faults were coldly condoned, his virtues as a poet were attacked, and his work was again mostly misunderstood by the reviewers. In 1882 the poet died, profoundly discouraged.

Fate has proved as unkind to Thomson's admirers as it had to the poet himself. Dobell's first posthumous collection of Thomson's poems, "A Voice from the Nile, and Other Poems," of 1884, resulted in another failure. A biography of Thomson by Henry S. Salt, published in 1889, was, despite William Shairp's loyal puff in the *Academy*, roundly abused by the magazine critics, and was in large part destroyed by a fire which also consumed almost all of Thomson's works previously unsold. A copy of the prose collection was saved, however, for the *Saturday Review* to comment upon in the following terms: "Had Thomson written in better papers and under more competent editorship, he would no doubt have learned to write prose better." Undeterred by these constant reverses, Dobell, in 1895, edited Thomson's Complete Poetical Works in two volumes, and in the following year published the first volume of his collected Critical Prose, intending three other volumes to follow it. The Poems attained a certain temporary success, but the first prose volume was so badly received that the three concluding volumes of the projected series were never attempted. Shortly afterwards, Reeves and Turner, who had published these various unsuccessful ventures for Dobell, went out of business. In the fall of 1914 Dobell himself died. Since his death, Thomson's fame has suffered a steady decline, broken only by the temporary and slight revivals of interest which attended a few other rare posthumous publications from his works. Mr. Salt's biography, owing alike to the coldness of the public and the fire at the printer's, is now a comparatively rare book. Thomson the poet would almost seem to have attained that

[ 3 ]

oblivion for which, as a man, he had so wistfully prayed.

This decline of Thomson's fame is commonly attributed not so much to the artistic shortcomings of the poet, as to the "unrelieved gloom" of his poetry. That this gloom is not all unrelieved, and that at its worst it is not an ignoble sort of pessimism, it is the purpose of the present volume later to demonstrate. Meanwhile the reader must admit that pessimism, "that strange disease of modern life," largely characterized most of the poets of the latter half of the last century. Browning's intense cheerfulness did not blind his eyes to such characters as Guido Caponsacchi. Tennyson was able to attain his grave moral happiness in life only after a great struggle, while Meredith saved himself from despair only by his strong will and his austere philosophy. Neither did the Pre-Raphaelites entirely escape into their art. Dante Rossetti walked in Willowwood almost all his life, Morris confessed his inability to "make quick-coming death a little thing," while Swinburne's prayer for absolute annihilation in the "Garden of Proserpine" was quite typical of his usual outlook on life. Arnold and Clough were openly and profoundly despondent.

Thomson is the most pessimistic of all these poets. Even Swinburne rarely touched such depths of despair as Thomson had explored in the *City of Dreadful Night:*

[ 4 ]

"Take a watch, erase
The signs and figures of the circling hours,
  Detach the hands, remove the dial-face;
The works proceed until run down, although
Bereft of purpose, void of use, still go."

Swinburne's popularity has without doubt been
greatly injured by the despairing gloom of the
*Poems and Ballads*. It is, therefore, little wonder that James Thomson, the extreme pessimist
of all these poets, should suffer at the hands of
the public for his dark philosophy.

Paradoxically enough, Thomson is by turns one
of the cheerfullest of all his poetic contempora-
ries. In many almost forgotten poems he is
delightfully rapturous, and in a manner quite
natural to his genius and temperament. Of his
life-long struggle between the deepest gloom and
this rich lyric delight in life, there is hardly any
realization in the popular mind. Thomson's
pessimism is not, therefore, the only reason for
his unpopularity. Neither is he an especially
faulty artist, for he was admired by some of the
keenest writers and critics of his day. The truth
is that Thomson was a radical in his life and his
connections. A Bohemian in the very respectable
Mid-Victorian period, he was entirely the antithe-
sis of Tennyson, the great popular poet of the
time. While he admired Tennyson's consummate art, Thomson despised his matter as

[ 5 ]

"hysterics and commonplace philosophy." He was utterly different from Longfellow, then the poetical demi-god of the middle classes, nor did he cloak his feelings toward the author of *Evangeline* in uncertain terms. "The sublime Excelsior," he once declared, explosively enough, "is very popular at present, but I doubt whether any man (soft curates, Sunday school teachers and tea meeting muffs who think beer and tobacco certain perdition, excepted) ever read the adventures of its lofty hero without ejaculating, 'The ineffable ass! The infernal idiot!'"

Such a writer, either as poet or as critic, was obviously not likely to enjoy too clamorous a public in those cautious and conservative days. Moreover, some of the "tea meeting muffs" struck back at Thomson in reviews and magazine articles. They declared that Thomson's failure in life was due to his cavalier manner in abandoning the teaching profession, and his willful refusal of "remunerative journalistic work on two great daily newspapers," with a comfortable salary and much leisure. Great stress has been laid by some of these "Sunday school teachers" on the poet's indulgence in the "artificial paradises induced by alcohol and drugs." They have charged Thomson with an inability to perform regular allotted tasks, and with a perverse insistence in working at literary jobs after his own heart. One reviewer of Thomson's second volume has even declared that the poet's pessimism in the *City of Dreadful Night* is purely an artifice—a literary trick! From the misunderstanding and neglect which he suffered at the hands of such contemporary critics as these, Thomson has never gained the popularity he deserves.

Thomson's poetry, as well as much of his prose, is inseparably connected with his life. He is one of the most personal of poets. While he was extremely reticent about discussing himself and his affairs, he put them nakedly and truthfully into his poems. His life was an incessant struggle with pessimism, and both his poems and his character must therefore be interpreted in terms of this struggle. Fortunately he dated all his poems and most of his prose with his own hand, and it is therefore not a difficult task to trace the progress of his actual and his spiritual life by studying his works in the order of their sequence. Although both Mr. Dobell and Mr. Salt, Thomson's two chief biographers, have suggested this method for investigating the poet's works, neither of them, curiously enough, has made any attempt at such a study. It is the purpose of the present essay to sketch the poet's life, using his poems and his prose chronologically as a key to his inner development.

## CHAPTER II

## YOUTH AND MATILDA (1834-1853)

JAMES THOMSON was born in Port-Glasgow on the twenty-third of November, 1834, of Scotch parents. The poet's double and contradictory nature came largely from his parents, who were utterly different from each other. His father was a captain in the merchant service, cheerful, bright, a clever mechanic and a good companion, who was especially fond of reading, reciting and singing. His mother, Sarah Kennedy, was deeply religious, strongly imaginative, and of a pensive, melancholy disposition. From the former the poet inherited that bonhomie and cheerful sociability which distinguished him all his life. From the latter he inherited his brooding imagination, his gloom and his emotional temperament. Owing to his mother, James was reared in a severely religious household. Edward Irving's portrait, covered with yellow gauze, hung in the parlor. The poet himself was as a little boy compelled to memorize the Assembly's Shorter Catechism, and was strictly dieted upon hymns and tracts popular with the Irvingites. So scrupulous was this early religious training that its influence clung to James all his days. His later blasphemies and slashes at orthodoxy are only the utterances of a deeply religious nature whose grim creed has completely failed him.

The poet's early childhood was not a happy one. He was barely able to remember the death of his younger and only sister. But in 1840 his father, while on a distant voyage, was paralyzed and rendered helpless mentally and physically until his death in 1853. Whether this stroke was the result of intemperance, of which the poet himself was later a victim and which, by his own admission, had run in his family, has been the subject of much fruitless discussion. The accident at once threw the family into financial distress, and in 1842 they appear at various addresses in East London, whither they had drifted. Thus the poet in his boyhood came to know the ugliness and murky atmosphere of the metropolis which he was destined later to describe in the *City of Dreadful Night:*

"The street lamps burn amidst the baleful
        glooms,
    Amidst the soundless solitudes immense
Of ranged mansions dark and still as tombs.
    The silence which benumbs and strains
        the sense

Fulfills with awe the soul's despair unweep-
    ing:
Myriads of habitants are ever sleeping,
Or dead, or fled from nameless pestilence!"

Although his later boyhood and early manhood
were for the most part spent in the country, nevertheless these grim, childish impressions of London never left him. His mother died in 1843,
leaving him to the care of his father, whose mind
wavered between fits of passionate anger or religious gloom, and the torpor of senility. Thomson, although usually very reticent about family
matters, once wrote the following impressions of
his childhood:

"I was just past eight years old and at
the school when mother died, so I can only
give you very early impressions. These are,
that father and mother were very happy
together when he was at home, until, when I
was about six, he returned from his last
voyage paralyzed in the right side, the result, as I understand, of a week of terrible
storm during which time he was never able
to change his drenched clothes. Before then
I think he was a good husband and a kind
father: her I always remember as a loving
mother and wife. He may have been gay, in
the sense of liking a social song and glass,
being, I believe, much better looking and

more attractive in company than either of his sons. She was more serious, and pious too, following Irving from the Kirk when he was driven out. I remember well Irving's portrait under yellow gauze, and some books of his on the interpretation of prophecy, which I used to read for the imagery. The paralysis at first unhinged father's mind, and he had some fits of violence; more generally his temper was strange, disagreeable, not to be depended upon. I remember him taunting her with being his elder. Mother must have had a sad time of it for a year or two. His mental perturbations settled down into a permanent weakness of mind, not amounting to imbecility, but very, very different, I should say, from his former brightness and decision. Before I went to the school he used to take me to chapels where the members of the congregation ejaculated groaning responses to the minister's prayer, and to small meetings in a private room where the members detailed their spiritual experiences for the week. Good, bad, or indifferent, those were not the things with which he had anything to do in his days of soundness. The right hand remained useless, but the leg had gradually grown strong enough to walk well, though with an awkward, dragging pace.

"I think mother, who was mystically inclined with Edward Irving, had also a cloud
of melancholy overhanging her; first, perhaps, from the death of her favorite brother,
John Parker Kennedy, drowned on the
Goodwin Sands; then probably deepened by
the death of my little sister, of whom I remember being devotedly fond, when she was
about three and myself five, of the measles
caught from me. Had she or someone else
lived, I might have been worth something;
but, on the whole, I sincerely judge that it
was well for both to die when they did, and
I would not, for my own selfish comfort,
call them back if I could. . . . Speaking generally, you know far more of my family than
I do, who have been Ishmael in the desert
from my childhood."

Fortunately, James was not entirely depend-
ent upon his father's care. Shortly before his
mother's death, he entered the Royal Caledonian
Asylum in London, his election there having been
procured by a Mr. J. Boyd, a former townsman
of his mother's. His career at this school, the
happiest period of his life, seems to have been
very successful. By his classmates he was remembered as "a fine, clever, high-spirited boy," a
leader in study and play. He impressed his
masters with his huge love of reading, and a de-

cided ability in mathematics. He early displayed his life-long love for music, which had been inherited from and developed by his father, for it is recorded that he played first clarionet in the school band.

In 1850 he found himself at the parting of the ways as to his future career. Lacking the money to gain a clerkship in business, which had been his original wish, he decided to fit himself for an army schoolmaster, and accordingly left the Royal Caledonian Asylum for the "Model School" in the Royal Military Asylum in Chelsea. Here also he became popular at once with his fellows, and displayed great ability as a student, owing alike to his powerful memory and to a natural aptitude for mathematics, an inheritance perhaps from his father, who in his time had been a clever mechanic. Even now the poet showed that breadth of literary taste, which was later to distinguish many critical essays still uncollected. His literary tastes developed early, as indeed did his whole mind. He read Shakespeare, Ben Jonson, Spenser, Milton, Fielding, Sterne, Smollett and De Foe. Swift and De Quincey, the strongest influences on his later prose, were already his favorite prose authors, while he now foreswore his worship of Byron, the idol of his youthful poetic enthusiasm, for Shelley, whose influence lasted all through his life.

During his holidays, Thomson used to visit the

Grays, old acquaintances of his father's, and came to be a great friend of the two daughters, Helen and Agnes. The latter has written her impressions of Thomson at this period in his life:

> "We always thought him wonderfully clever, very nice-looking, and very gentle, grave and kind. . . . My eldest sister (Helen) was his especial favorite. Her will always seemed law to him. She was gay as he was grave, but whatever Helen said or did won appreciation from him. . . . Previous to going (to Ireland) he earnestly requested that my sister might be allowed to correspond with him, a request which my parents thought it wise to refuse."

Thomson proved to be a methodical, industrious student, and mastered several languages entirely by his own exertions. The breadth and acuteness of his literary tastes are shown by the fact that in 1850 he was already reading Browning and Meredith, who at that time were being quite neglected by the public. A most promising career seemed in store for him.

In the summer of 1851 Thomson left the Military Asylum at Chelsea in order to learn the practical duties of the army schoolmaster, for which he had been fitting himself. He was sent to Ballincollig, near Cork, as assistant to the garrison master, a Mr. Joseph Barnes. For the next two years he taught there in the regimental school. He was considered by his master a brilliant and accomplished assistant, and, in spite of his seventeen years, showed himself entirely qualified to teach. Barnes was a self-educated and kindly man. Both he and his wife became warm friends of Thomson, and did everything in their power to make his life at Ballincollig pleasant and enjoyable. For the first time in his life Thomson lived within the intimacy of a normal and affectionate family. In a series of six sonnets written in 1862, Thomson commemorates his sincere affection for the Barneses. Yet it was here that he was destined to experience the supreme delight and the supreme tragedy of his life—a tragedy with consequences so great that his promising abilities came to nothing but a few of the saddest and most terrible poetic masterpieces to which our literature can lay claim.

Matilda Weller was the beautiful daughter of an armorer-sergeant then stationed at Ballincollig. Years afterwards, in his fantastic *Vane's Story,* Thomson described her:

"For thought retraced the long, sad years
  Of pallid smiles and frozen tears
  Back to a certain festal night,
  A whirl and blaze of swift delight
  When we together danced, we two;
  I live it all again—Do you

Remember how I broke down quite
In the mere polka? . . . Dressed in white,
A loose pink sash around your waist,
Low shoes across the instep laced,
Your moon-white shoulders glancing through
Long yellow ringlets dancing too,
You were an angel then; as clean
From earthly dust-speck, as serene
And lovely and above my love
As now in your far world above."

This is Thomson's usual description of Matilda—young and pure, dressed in white and pink, with yellow ringlets. Mr. Salt states that he verified this description through a daguerreotype which in 1889 was in the possession of William Weller, a relative.

When the poet first met Matilda at the Barnes', she was barely fourteen, and he himself only eighteen. Yet Thomson's passion for her was not a superficial one, as two terrible cantos of the *City of Dreadful Night,* written over twenty years afterwards, will attest. Thomson, like many other poets who have loved young, was noted for his precocity, and in fact bore the pet name "Co" in the Barnes household. Unusual as such a youthful attachment is, there is no reason whatsoever to consider it as a mere literary motif for his later years. In the *Fadeless Bower,* written in 1858, a half-forgotten poem whose lulls are

[ 16 ]

reminiscent of the rich, sensuous details and liquid undertones of Rossetti, but whose more fervid stanzas have a powerful sincerity which the Pre-Raphaelites rarely possessed, Thomson has described his love-plight with his "Good Angel":

"Behold her as she standeth there,
    Breathless, with fixed, awe-shadowed
      eyes
  Beneath her moon-touched golden hair!
    Her spirit's poor humilities
  Are trembling, half would disavow
  The crown I bring to crown her brow.

"The simplest folds of white invest
    Her noble form, as purest snow
  Some far and lovely mountain-crest
    Faint-flushed with all the dawn's first
      glow,
  Alone, resplendent, lifted high
  Into the clear, vast, breathless sky.

\*     \*     \*     \*     \*

"Could that one hour have been drawn out
    Until the end of Time's whole range!
  We rapt away, so sphered about,
    And made eternal, free from change;
  In heart and mind, in soul and frame
  Preserved for evermore the same!

\*     \*     \*     \*     \*

"Entranced above the worded Yes
 All flushed and pale with rapturous
  shame,
In that dim moonlit quietness
 You stand for evermore the same,
Fairer than heaven, the Queen who now
Is trembling as I crown her brow."

It is not actually known whether the two young
lovers became formally engaged, for Thomson
never alluded to the affair afterward, except in his
poems. Apart from the evidence in the last
stanza quoted above, both Mr. Dobell and Mr.
Salt express no doubts that Thomson's suit was
approved by the girl's parents, as the poet seemed
a most clever and promising young man to everyone at that time. His love for Matilda was certainly well known to the Barnes family, and his
engagement to her was apparently accepted by
them as an obvious fact. For a little time, at
least, there was nothing to cloud their happiness,
and the poet's almost life-long melancholia seems
to have been lifted from his mind.

Thomson remained in Ballincollig for the
greater part of two years to gain practice in
teaching, after which he returned to Chelsea.
This step marked the beginning of a series of
final studies before Thomson became a full-
fledged schoolmaster. This routine was scarcely
necessary in his case, as he was already well quali-

fied, and it seems to have irked him much. In *Love's Dawn,* his only poem written in 1852, we find the young poet dreaming of his mistress across the Irish Sea, in a highly personal and significant manner, although somewhat in the style of Browning's *Pauline:*

"Still thine eyes haunt me; in the darkness
    now,
  The dreamtime, the hushed stillness of the
    night
  I see them shining, pure and earnest light;
  And here, all lonely, may I not avow
  The thrill with which I ever meet their
    glance?
  At first they gazed a calm, abstracted gaze,
  The while thy soul was floating through
    some maze
  Of beautiful divinely-peopled trance;
  But now I shrink from them in shame and
    fear,
  For they are gathering all their beams of
    light
  Into an arrow, keen, intense, and bright,
  Swerveless and starlike from its deep blue
    sphere,
  Piercing the cavernous darkness of my soul,
  Burning its foul recesses into view;
  Transfixing with sharp agony through and
    through

Whatever is not brave and clean and whole.
And yet I will not shrink, although thou piercest
      piercest
Into the inmost depths of all my being:
I will not shrink, although thou art now seeing
      seeing
My heart's caged lusts, the wildest and the fiercest;
      fiercest;
The cynic thoughts that fret my homeless mind,
      mind,
My unbelief, my selfishness, my weakness,
My dismal lack of charity and meekness;
For, amidst all the evil, thou wilt find
Pervading, cleansing and transmuting me,
A fervent and most holy love for Thee."

During this separation from Matilda, almost all that was fairest and noblest in life became in Thomson's mind indissolubly linked with her ever present image. To him, with his constant tendency toward allegory, she grew to be an almost sacred symbol. His prospects during this second stay at Chelsea were very bright. He had acquired no little knowledge of books, and had seen something of men and the world. He had won the love of a beautiful girl, and had succeeded brilliantly at Ballincollig as an assistant. Thus far he had shown himself unusually capable, and was well liked by all his acquaintances. For the first time in his life he seemed on the point of earning a competent living. Perhaps had the tremendous inspiration of her presence been always his, Thomson would never have paced the ghostly streets in that "most dolent city." Perhaps his melancholia would have lifted and been dispersed, like the wisps of fog under the radiance of the sunshine. So at least the poet himself thought in the *Fadeless Bower*, and in many other pathetic poems of his later life. Yet the price of great poetry is human pain, and this happiness was not destined for him. Already had "Melancholy marked him for her own."

Matilda died in the early summer of 1853, when the poet had almost finished his studies at Chelsea. It has been conjectured from his prose masterpiece, *A Lady of Sorrow*, that the poet knew her to be in frail health, and had perhaps a natural apprehension for her death, which Fate converted into a seeming prophecy:

"One whom I scarcely know whether to call friend or enemy; she who came suddenly (though indeed her advent had been long before announced) in the brilliant morning of a joyous summer holiday to dwell with me and possess me; permitting no rivals nor any approach to rivalry, absorbing every thought and feeling to her devotion, and compelling even the dreams and visions of both night and day to worship her."

Whether anticipated or not, however, he received a letter one morning telling of her dangerous illness, and the next day the news of her death came to him. The death of Matilda was to prove the most momentous event in his whole life. It is beside the point to conjecture whether this bereavement was the actual cause of his later life-long sorrow, or whether it was merely a supreme incident to which his inevitable melancholy attached itself. The shock of her death the poet has again and again recorded, sometimes with pathos, as in the *Fadeless Bower,* and sometimes with grim tragedy, as in the *City*. In the *Lady of Sorrow* he wrote:

> "I speak not of her, I cannot speak of her, as she came at first; when my spirit was stunned and lay as dead in the body mechanically alive; lay in swoon with but the dimmest consciousness of her presence, sitting down black-veiled beside me many nights and days, speaking not a word, as the friends of Job sat silent at first, for they saw that his grief was very great."

He never forgot her. The very year he died, Thomson was writing of her still. While the other interests of his life, his career, his religion, his health, and even his art, all slowly withered away, her image remained always radiant and always poignant with the beauty of the days that are no more. In his happier moments he could wistfully dream of what might have been, and in a pathetic mockery live out for some brief hours a shadowy life of love.

"For she was simply the image in beatitude of her who died so young. The pure girl was become an angel; the sheathed wings had unfolded in the favorable clime, the vesture was radiantly white with the whiteness of her soul, the long hair was a dazzling glory around the ever-young head, the blue eyes had absorbed celestial light in the cloudless empyrean: but still, thus developed and beautiful, she was only the more intensely and supremely herself; more perfectly revealed to me, more intimately known and more passionately loved by me, than when she had walked the earth in the guise of a mortal. She would take me by the hand, sometimes impressing a kiss, which was an ample anodyne, upon my world-weary brow, and lead me away floating calmly through the infinite height and depth and breadth; from galaxy to galaxy, from silver star to star."

The inevitable comparison of the above passage to Dante's supreme vision of Beatrice, and

"L'amor chi move il sol e l'altre stelle," is not merely accidental, for in many aspects both the life and the poems of Thomson resemble the immortal Florentine's more closely than any other English poet. But on the other hand, while Thomson's grimmer moods were upon him, this memory of Matilda could embody to him all the supreme loveliness of the world, which in life's tragic pageant was doomed by the "blind gods who cannot spare." Thus we find her wraith enduring in the *City of Dreadful Night* and the perfume of her departed presence even amid the horror of *In the Room*. None of the biographers who knew the poet, and no reputable critic who knew his poems, has ever seriously questioned Thomson's sincerity in this tragic afterglow of his love for Matilda Weller. Into every prose and poetic masterpiece that he wrote, this memory of her love is subtly but unfailingly woven. With her death, he too began a "new life."

# CHAPTER III

## STUDY AND TEACHING (1853-1862)

AFTER the initial torpor of his grief for Matilda had subsided, Thomson went about his studies outwardly the same. During 1853 he wrote nothing. He did finish his studies at Chelsea, however, and in August, 1854, about the time of the Crimean War, he enlisted as army schoolmaster to a militia regiment in Devonshire. This was but the first of many posts which he occupied during the next eight years. He was frequently shifted, and taught successively at Aldershot, Dublin, Curragh Camp, again at Aldershot, and at Portsmouth. In those days a schoolmaster in the English army was considered a soldier rather than a civilian. Thomson wore the uniforms of the respective regiments to which he was attached, and was, theoretically at least, obliged to conform to the usual military discipline. He taught children in the morning and the soldiers in the afternoon, besides additional instruction during the evening to pupils who were either too rapid or too slow for the regular classes. On the whole, Thomson proved to be an efficient teacher, owing to his keen, clear intellect and to his methodical, industrious habits. Yet his heart was not in the work. Thomson was popular with his associates and with the soldiers, without being intimate with any of them. Outwardly he was cheerful and genial, in an occupation which he described to a friend as "Pumping muddy information into un-retentive sieves." Inwardly, and during those leisure hours when he most truly lived, he was passing through a great spiritual struggle, and as an artist was serving his apprenticeship in verse, of which he wrote much during these years. Thomson's Bohemian ways were greatly encour-aged by this rough, shifting life, and his lack of friends threw his mind back upon itself and its memories. One advantage, at least, he gained from it—a knowledge of nature and of country life. There is a richness of color and a sense of beauty in these poems of his early years which are more rarely found after he had returned to live in London. Yet in even these later poems there are many natural touches which his observing mind had garnered while he was in Ireland or at Portsmouth.

As might be expected, his only poem in 1854 was a lament for Matilda, and was entitled, *Marriage*. In the following year he wrote the *Dreamer,* which also deals with the poet's dreams of marriage with his dead lady, and the reflec-tion (a trifle uncertain, it seems) that she was in a better world. In a poem *Suggested by Matthew*

*Arnold's "Stanzas from the Grand Chartreuse"*
he laments the departure of the old, comforting
faith, and disparages the arrogance of modern
science, the sordidness of Mammon-worship, and
the sentimental worship of poverty by humanitarians. Most significant, however, is the fact
that his old orthodoxy is now shattered, and he
finds himself groping in the dark, painfully unable
to believe the old creed, to which, however, he is
not yet hostile. In 1856 he wrote his *Tasso to
Leonora,* in which the poet shows his apprehension as to the immortality of the soul, and again
reveals the scars of his unhappy love affair.

The year of 1857 was his first great productive
year in poetry, and because of the fact, it shows
the two sides of the poet's nature; one, the cheerful and even rapturous good fellow; the other, the
gloomy, anxious dreamer whose love is dead. At
times Thomson was able to enter into the rough
army life about him, as is shown by several army
poems published this year; the *Capstan Chorus,*
the *Jolly Veterans,* and the *Sergeant's Mess Song.*
In their occasional touches of realistic good humor, these poems remind the reader oddly of the
*Barrack Room Ballads.* Yet the second of these
poems ends in a fatalistic spirit which reveals the
other and darker side of Thomson's temperament. The subject of *Bertram to the Lady
Geraldine* was no doubt suggested by Mrs.
Browning's more famous poem. Here we see his

unforgotten vision of love struggling with fatalism, and triumphing over it. Again he recalls, as later in *Vane's Story*, the rapture of the dance with his beloved:

"Oh, glory of the dance sublimed to this!
Oh, pure white arm electric that embraced
Ethereal-lightly my unbounded bliss!
Oh, let me die but in another taste
Of that warm breath ambrosial, and the kiss
Of those whirl-wanton ringlets; interlaced
Quick frame with frame borne on; my lips the while
Within a neck-bend of that heavenly smile!"

This is not the description of the Lady Geraldine—it is again his memory of Matilda, expressed with the uncertain technique of a young poet. Here, as before in *Tasso to Leonora*, the poet seizes upon an old love story as a vehicle for his personal experiences and moods. At the end love triumphs:

"Be pain unnoticed in a doom like this!
I see eyes gazing on my weary night
Like cold, strange stars from out the world-abyss;

[ 28 ]

They gaze with scorn or pity; but their
       sight
Is banished from my inward golden bliss,
  Floating divinely in the noonday light
Of thee round whom I circle—O far Sun
Through mirk and slime alike the earth's
       true course is run!"

Yet the triumph of his love is something of a
Pyrrhian victory. Against the bitter fate with
which he struggles, he opposes now passionate
idealism, and now only faltering and wistful
rhetoric.

In the *Festival of Life,* written the next month,
Thomson's imagination, for the first time recorded in his verse, fully took fire. The poem is
an allegorical narrative in free ode-stanzas, after
Shelley. There is in it much sweeping lyric power
and much highly imaginative description. Like
some of the allegories of Shelley, too, it is rather
difficult to interpret. It seems to be an allegorical
restatement of the poet's spiritual experiences,
in which his artistic nature and his love of song
and beauty struggle with the inevitable sense of
Doom. The poet relates how, at a riotous feast,
the banqueters are startled and sobered by the
entrance of two mysterious masquers, who at each
appearance carry off one of the revellers. These
masquers seem to represent Death in its double
aspect of a gracious deliverer and as a malignant

demon. In passages it is as finely descriptive as anything that Thomson ever wrote:

> "The lamps were quickly failing;
> The pictures were weird shadows on the
> wall;
> In the grey stone-cold, dawn-gleams unpre-
> vailing
> The draperies seemed a vast funeral pall
> Flapping about the corpse like sculpture
> wan;
> The floor, the cupola which glimmering
> shone,
> The rain-dark marbles in the tempest
> thrilled;
> Where the noble feast was spread
> Lay scattered flower-blooms, dim and
> dead,
> Mid streams of sullen-oozing wine outspilled
> From urns and goblets in a sick confusion
> strown;
> And lost in all the ghastly waste,
> On couches tottering and displaced,
> Flushed victims of the orgy, helpless, sense-
> less, prone."

Under a religious and moral veil, the allegory of which suggests Poe's *Masque of the Red Death,* Thomson shows in this poem a terrible despair on contemplating death. While the Good and the Beautiful conquer, there is a doubtful air about their victory, as though the poet were trying rather to persuade himself of the triumph than to celebrate it.

The influence of Shelley is again seen, and even more clearly, in Thomson's first poetic masterpiece, the *Doom of a City,* a lyric allegory founded on Zobeide's tale of the Petrified City, in the "Arabian Nights." In style this poem is very like the *Festival of Life,* only on a considerably larger scale. It is no trifling indication of Thomson's precocity that he could have written so good a poem at twenty-three.

The *Doom of a City* is in four main parts. The first recounts how despair drives a poet to embark alone in a boat, and after a long voyage beset by rather incomprehensible monsters, who in Thomson's mind probably represented religious fears, to land in a strange stone city. This section of the poem resembles Shelley's *Alastor* in its rambling voyage-structure, and in many of its mysterious allegorical incidents. Thomson himself realized that it was prolix, yet he refused to change or omit it.

In the second part, there is a description of this city, where all life has turned to stone—an allegory of the stony insensibility of the human heart when numbed by destiny and despair. It is this section which most strongly suggests the *City of Dreadful Night,* except that this city is of sense-

less stone, while that is a ghastly night-vision of a
living, moving metropolis:

> "What found I?—Dead stone sentries stony-
> eyed,
> Erect, steel-sworded, brass-defended all,
> Guarding the sombrous gateway deep and
> wide
> Hewn like a cavern through the mighty
> wall;
> Stone statues all throughout the streets and
> squares
> Grouped as in social converse or alone;
> Dim stony merchants holding forth rich
> wares
> To catch the choice of purchasers of stone;

*　　*　　*　　*　　*

> "Over the bridge's sculptured parapet;
> Statues in boats, amidst its sway and quiver
> Immovable as if in ice-waves set:—
> The whole vast sea of life about me lay,
> The passionate, heaving, restless, sounding
> life,
> With all its tides and billows, foam and
> spray,
> Arrested in full tumult of its strife
> Frozen into a nightmare's ghastly death,
> The vigorous heart and brain and blood
> and breath
> Stark, strangled, coffined in eternal stone."

[ 32 ]

The climax of the poem, "The Judgment," comes in the third section of the poem, where the narrator overhears God's Doom on the City. In this Judgment, which has somehow the hall-marks of early inflicted Scotch Presbyterianism about it, and whose manner is constantly reminiscent of Shelley and De Quincey, the wicked statues crash to dust, and the good become free spirits. In conclusion there is a triumph-song of these liberated spirits, which indicates that Thomson had not yet wholly cast off the old orthodoxy:

"As one who in the morning-shine
    Reels homeward, shameful, wan, adust,
From orgies wild with fiery wine
    And reckless sin and brutish lust:
And sees a doorway open wide,
    And then the grand Cathedral space
And hurries in to crouch and hide
    His trembling frame, his branded face.

    *      *      *      *      *

"He sees the world-wide morning flame
    Through windows where in glory shine
The saints who fought and overcame,
    The martyrs who made death divine:
He sees pure women bent in prayer,
    Communing low with God above:—
*Too* pure! what right has *he* to share
    Their silent feast of sacred love?"

The fourth part, "The Return," is calmer and more didactic in tone. Thomson here states his creed of life vaguely and uncertainly, but not without force and art. Like Shelley he considers organized social institutions, such as the government and the church, as tyrannous and soulless machines. Their adherents, he thinks, are clinging blindly to the symbol and forgetting the spiritual forces which the symbol was created to represent. Yet unlike Shelley or Leopardi, Thomson had no strong constructive vision of the elements which must be built up to replace these outworn institutions. In his fierce invective he has drawn so grim and sombre a background for his idealism, that his positive and more hopeful beliefs are engulfed by the shadows of it. The poem reveals the poet's religious views in their deepening development. Despite some lines of noble certainty, there is the same doubtful and wistful rhetoric about his statement of his belief in the immortality of the human soul, and the benevolence of an overruling God. Here, as later in the *Lady of Sorrow,* he is tortured by fatalism, and ponders on the transmigration of souls. Years after, in the highly biographical *Vane's Story,* Thomson stated very frankly the spiritual agony through which he was passing at this time:

"I half remember, years ago,
  Fits of despair that maddened woe,

Frantic remorse, intense self scorn,
And yearnings harder to be borne
Of utter loneliness forlorn;
What passionate secret prayers I prayed!
What futile firm resolves I made!
As well a thorn might pray to be
Transformed into an olive tree;
The *I am that I am* of God
Defines no less a worm or clod,
My penitence was honest guile;
My inmost being all the while
Was laughing in a patient mood
At this extreme solicitude,
Was waiting laughing till once more
I should be sane as heretofore;
And in the pauses of the fits
That rent my heart and scared my wits,
Its pleasant mockery whispered through,
*Oh, what can Saadi have to do*
*With penitence? and what can you?*
*And Shiraz roses wreathed with rue?"*

So, torn between his artistic delight in beauty, his pangs as a fatalist and a hopeless lover, and his mocking laughter at the incongruity of his feelings about both, his first great creative year passed. He wrote other and less significant poems this year also: *The Purple Flower of the Heath,* a romantic ballad-tragedy set in the Middle Ages of the Gothic revival; *A Chant* and

*Withered Leaves,* both exquisite but rather tenuous laments; and a highly biographical poem written on his twenty-third birthday, which was never included in the collected editions of his works, but which is the key to the *Festival of Life* and the *Doom of a City* in its confessional frankness. He seems melancholy alike over his wasted years and his apparently hopeless future. He finds the dull routine of his life almost intolerable. He can likewise realize the subtle temptations and inevitable perils of dissipation. Yet the poem ends with a trumpet-call to the fight which defies even Fate itself. This refusal to submit is what makes Thomson's life and his poems so nobly tragic. Even at the end of that terrible masterpiece, the *City of Dreadful Night,* the reader finds him defiant, as he was at twenty-three:

"Meanwhile, then, let me wait and hope, and learn
    To curb with galling steel and ruthless hand
These strong and passionate impulses that burn
    To sweep me from my post of self-command
Into the battle raging thick and stern,
    Into the desert's freedom vast and grand;

That horseman proves full strength, firm
    skill indeed,
Who holdeth statue-calm his savage steed."

The outward events of this period of the poet's
life were few and colorless. Occasional letters
written by him to Agnes Gray in 1858 reveal, in
spite of their vivacious style, a monotonous existence of routine and hearsay, rather than inde-
pendent action:

    " . . . your humble servant has spent six
weeks in another Barracks since he had the
honor of writing you last, and is now attached
to the 55th Foot. Whither this noble corps
will be sent no one just now ventures to guess.
Lately, vague rumors were afloat of its
transportation to India. Probably, however,
a tender government would preserve the
precious dominie, even when banishing his
regiment. One of our class died out there
not long since—a thin, wiry fellow who
promised to endure all climates with the sal-
low tenacity of parchment. . . . With regard to the Piano, I shall indeed be rejoiced
to hear you playing some fine day, but, for
myself, I am utterly innocent of the art."

The year 1858 did not prove so productive of
poetry as 1857. Thomson wrote this year the

*Fadeless Bower,* a narrative verse autobiography
of his unforgotten love affair, and the alternate
torture and exaltation which its memory afforded
him. It is perhaps the tenderest and most pensive of Thomson's poems, and appeared in *Tait's
Edinburgh Review* for July, over the signature of
"Crepusculus." This is only one of many poems
which the lonely army schoolmaster now began to
contribute to the minor magazines of the time,
such as Bradlaugh's *London Investigator,* and
later his *National Reformer.* Thomson about this
time adopted the pen-name, "Bysshe Vanolis," or,
as he generally printed it, "B. V." So consistently
did he employ this *nom de plume* in print, that
admirers like Dobell had at first no knowledge of
the poet's real name. The same year that marks
Thomson's entry into periodical literature also
includes the production of a few minor but inter-
esting poems, such as the *Requiem,* the *Winter's
Night, Cypress and Roses,* the biographical *At
Death's Door* and the *Recusant,* which is the
poet's last regretful yearning for the comfortable repose of the Christian church. Hereafter
Thomson is not gracious, but fiercely indignant
with the orthodox creed, with an ironic bitterness
which betrays his severe youthful experiences with
religion. Thomson was never an unreligious
man, and could never forget religious questions
for long. Henceforward he is either sorrowing
over the beauties of a consolation from which he

finds himself debarred, or else he is savagely irreverent at what to him is a deceptive and mocking delusion.

Thomson spent 1859 with his regiment in Ireland. In letters to various friends he has left a vivid picture of this rough and ready life, in which he mixed as a boon and cheerful companion, and yet which occupied only the fringes of his mind:

"The move has come, and we are now settled in this camp. Imagine an undulating sea of grass, here and there rising into hillocks, and spotted with patches of flowerless furze. In the midst, on a slightly elevated ridge, stretches for about a mile the camp, consisting of ten squares of dingy red huts— each square holding a regiment—with a somewhat irregular accompaniment of canteens, wash-houses, hospitals, huts for the staff, etc. In the center of a line, chosen probably as the highest spot, stands the Church, the Chapel (Roman Catholic) and the Clock-tower: at the extremities are the white tents of artillery and Dragoons. It is a fine place for freedom and expanse, and in itself much pleasanter than Aldershot, though I could wish to be there for the sake of its nearness to London. Aldershot is set amidst dark heath, the Curragh amidst green grass, and the difference is like that between cloudy and sunshiny weather. It is good to get out here from a town. The sky is seen, not in patches, but broad, complete and sea-like; the distance where low blue hills float in the horizon is also sea-like, and the incorrupted air sweeps over us broad and free as an ocean. . . . I have very good quarters for the camp, better probably than most of the officers. Two rooms, one of them papered, forming the end of the school hut, are something to boast of for a habitation.

"The camp is now about full. Between two and three miles off is the village of Newbridge, a cavalry station. Here and there the troopers must number nearly ten thousand men. So that with the assistance of those in Dublin, we ought to get up a good 'Field-day' or Review for Her Majesty, should she come over, as is expected. Lord Seaton, the Commander-in-Chief for Ireland, is here, with all sorts of generals, staff-officers and aides-de-camp. I wish you could have seen the whole division the other day, as they marched past before the great man. The Horse Artillery careering as if their guns were cabs and carriages; the more sober Foot-Artillery and Military Train; the Scots Grays with their bearskins like mounted Guardsmen; the Royal Dragoons, brass-helmeted; the 5th Irish Lancers looking splendid, like chivalry of old, with lances erect, and each topped with its red and white pennon; then regiment after regiment of infantry, including a battalion of the Fusilier Guards; each corps marching past to the music of its own band, the Fusiliers having their bagpipes. Then there were aides-de-camp and regimental field-officers galloping about in all directions, swift and brilliant as butterflies; mere butterflies, many of them, but very pleasant and exciting to look at."

The poems written in 1859 show the same curious alternation between cheerful aspiration, and the fatalistic sorrow of the pessimist. *A Happy Poet* is perhaps the most objective poem he ever composed. Here Thomson feels that all the pageant of humanity, sorrowful or joyous by turns, is apart from him because of his position as an observing artist:

"How vast the stage!
Imperious Doom, unvanquishable will,
Throughout the Drama constant battle
    wage;
The plot evolves with tangled good and
    ill;
The passions overflood the Shores of Time;
With God the full solution waits sublime."

Had Thomson usually possessed this power of looking at the world objectively, he would have been far less pessimistic in his general feeling toward life.  As it was, he brooded over his own emotions and ideas to such a dangerous extent that his consciousness turned upon itself, and the sombre pessimism of the *City* resulted.  The escape from this tragic mood lay partly in his creative artistic powers, as he saw himself in a later stanza of *A Happy Poet*:

"For I must sing of all I feel and know;
  Waiting with Memnon passive near the
    palms,
 Until the heavenly light doth dawn and
    glow
 And thrill my silence into mystic psalms;
 From unknown realms the wind streams
    sad or gay,
  The trees give voice responsive to its
    sway."

The Poet of this poem, who of course is only Thomson in one of his happier moods, feels that life is good and beautiful, and that he can find happiness in singing its praises.  This attractive program, however, he was never destined consistently to fulfill.

Much the same cheerful philosophy, however, appears in another poem written in 1859, the

*Lord of the Castle of Indolence,* in the old Spen-
serian stanzas of his better known namesake.
Into the dreamy sweetness of the stanza there is
introduced a calm Oriental resignation, and a
strand or two of the inevitable fatalism:

> "How men will strain to row against the
> tide,
>> Which yet must sweep them down in its
>> career;
> Or if some win their way and crown their
> pride
>> What do they win? the desert wild and
>> drear,
>> The savage rocks, the icy wastes
>> austere."

While the indifference to the future in this poem
is not characteristic of Thomson's commoner and
deeper theories of both life and art, yet it does
reveal a careless, indolent side to his nature which
many phases of his life and of his poems bear
witness to, as for example his essay on *Indolence.*
Yet for the most part he was destined to the
nobler though more tragic life of those who
"strain to row against the tide."

*An Old Dream,* another poem written in 1859,
is done in imitation of the *Blessed Damosel.*
Where Rossetti was unconsciously prophesying
the death of his beloved, however, Thomson nar-

rates an actual experience. He preserves the
same hushed, sweet music, and there is none of his
usual rapturous delight or fiery indignation in it.
It is not so much a poem of personal feeling as
of subtly beautiful atmosphere:

> "And up the music-moonlit sea
>     They floated calm and slow,
> So that it rather seemed to be
>     The earth was sinking low
> Than that they soared, so steadfastly
>     Ascending they did go."

In the *Deliverer* Thomson relates, with more
personal feeling and lyric intensity, the saving
values of his vision of Matilda, to his gloomy,
oppressed mind. The *Real Vision of Sin* was
written in irritation at Tennyson's languidly beautiful *Vision of Sin,* which to Thomson was utterly
artificial and insincere. The Scotchman's instinct
for truth prompted him here to draw a hideous
picture of real sin. But the account of this poetic
year is incomplete without mention of *Mater
Tenebrarum,* an outburst of sensuous anguish at
his bereavement. The gathering gloom and
increasing melancholy of his nature here find a
fiery Swinburnian utterance. He cries out in the
night at the thought that perhaps his love is dead
in soul as well as body:

"In the endless nights, from my bed, where
    sleepless in frenzy I lie,
I cleave through the crushing gloom with a
    bitter and deadly cry:
Oh! where have they taken my Love from
    our Eden of bliss on this earth,
Which now is a frozen waste of sepulchral
    and horrible dearth?
Have they killed her indeed? is her soul as
    her body, which long
Has mouldered away in the dust where the
    foul worms throng?
O'er what abhorrent Lethes, to what re-
    motest star,
Is she rapt away from my pursuit thru'
    cycles and systems far?
She is dead, she is utterly dead; for her life
    would hear and speed
To the wild imploring cry of my heart that
    cries in its dreadful need."

Thomson finds

"No hope in this worn-out world, no hope
    beyond the tomb;
No living and loving God, but blind and
    stony Doom."

For the first time recorded in his poems, he is
half minded to commit suicide and end it all. Yet
here, as later, there remains in him:

[ 45 ]

"A fire of dread, a light of hope, kindled, O
        Love, by thee;
For thy pure and gentle and beautiful soul,
        it must immortal be."

It is just this unquenchable glimmer of hope that
prevented his suicide always, that lent nobility to
his life struggle, and genius to his most pessimistic poems.

The details of the poet's life during 1860 are
as shadowy as during 1858 or 1859. Most of his
correspondence seems to have been with Agnes
Gray, and in his usual bantering tone:

"How have I offended you by irreverent
allusions to our Future Abode? By saying
that you will go to heaven? that I shall go?
that we shall meet there? that you will play
the harp there? that I shall hear you harp-
playing there? that your said harp-playing
there will afford a criterion of your piano-
forte-playing here? that I shall be able to
apply this criterion there? By which or by
all, have I shocked you? . . . I beseech
pardon.

"Miss Helen shocks me. Twenty-four
pounds sterling scarcely sufficient to keep her
in dress! I think that teachers in Ragged
Schools should go clothed in rags, humbling
themselves in sympathy with their scholars,

and thus winning their confidence.  How can tattered fustian and cotton believe that silk and lace have any affection for them? . . . However, I give up the scheme on account of the sweetheart.  I suppose she will soon be married, for after profound calculation, I have discovered that she is three or four months over twenty. . . . As for you, most venerable of women, you will be eighteen next month, will you not?  I wish the world would stand still a while, and not bring on grey hairs at this alarming rate.

"My good friends Mr. and Mrs. Barnes expect to go to London soon, he as Garrison Schoolmaster there.  Please ask Mr. and Mrs. Gray if I may give the Barneses a note of introduction to you all.  They are really good people.  Mr. B. is clever, intelligent, full of fun and humor, honest, kindly and genial.  I am bound to confess that his conversation is dashed with that roughness to which we unfortunates, knocked about hither and thither into involuntary intimacy with each other in the Army, get, and must get, pretty well used to. . . .

"Mrs. Barnes I like even better.  She is very reserved at first, but quite motherly and womanly when one gets to know her well.  Both have treated me with great and rare kindness."

The year 1860 proved a lull in Thomson's poetic career. He wrote only four poems that have survived, and three of these were occasional. The *Two Sonnets,* wherein he is thinking of himself and his fate, reveal his attitude toward his art. He finds that his songs are all sad, but that only in sadness can he attain true poetry. The concluding couplet is epigrammatic, and remarkably truthful:

"My mirth can laugh and talk, but cannot
sing;
My grief finds harmonies in everything."

Outwardly, no doubt, Thomson was the same witty and engaging comrade that he had always been. Yet his growing melancholy he now recognized as his sincerest and most powerful impulse.

Thomson was shifted in 1860 from Curragh Camp to Aldershot, a change for which he was apparently grateful, as Ireland had come to be a land of painful memories to him. Also, he now found himself near to his childhood friends, the Grays, to whom he at once paid a visit which had rather significant results. It must be remembered that before going to Ireland, Thomson had been quite intimate with Helen Gray, and had corresponded with her. In September, 1860, when he called on the family, he found her engaged. His visit has been described by Agnes Gray (Mrs. Grieg), the younger sister:

"At last he wrote saying that he was to have a fortnight's holiday, and would pay us a visit. We were all excitement at his coming. I had previously informed him in one of my letters that Helen had become a Ragged School teacher, and in reply he said that he could not imagine a creature so bright and in his remembrance so beautiful being arrayed in sombre habiliments, and acting such a character. . . . During this visit we thought him much altered in appearance and manners, indeed, we were somewhat disappointed. He was by no means so manly looking as when he left London, and was painfully silent and depressed. He went from us with the intention of again going to Aldershot, but from that day until Mr. Maccall mentioned him to us, we never once heard of him. Ever since we have felt greatly puzzled to account for his singular conduct."

Thomson's remissness, which the Grays could not understand, is no puzzle to us now. They probably knew nothing of his lost love at Ballincollig, and his usual reticence in talking about himself or his depression probably deepened the mystery to them. Yet there was another element in his attitude which brought on melancholy during his stay at their home, and which probably caused his unexpected silence afterward. This was a brief but intense revival of his early love for Helen Gray, which is shown in the sad and obviously sincere *Meeting Again*:

> "And now again, after long bitter years,
>     We are allowed to meet
> And mingle henceforth all our sighs and
>         tears
>     While these two hearts shall beat.
>
> \*      \*      \*      \*      \*
>
> "Ah! can you really love me, whom you
>         know
>     So weak and foul of yore?
> Dear Heart! *I* feel that evil long-ago
>     But makes me love you more.
>
> "Yet still that longing almost swayeth me—
>     That we should sink down deep,
> And side by side, from life's sore burden
>         free,
>     Sleep death's eternal sleep."

Thomson was thus torn between two impossible affections—one, that life-long and passionate reverence for the dead Matilda, and the other, this rebirth of an earlier love for a woman already engaged to marry another. It is only natural that Thomson should have tried to put Helen Gray out of mind, for she could not be his, despite the pathetic hope of his melancholy poem.

Moreover, it must have been painful to him to feel that he was blurring the memory of Matilda, for this had come to be the lodestone of all his dreams and hopes. His way out of the difficulty—to avoid their house and all correspondence with them—was in reality the noblest and best, however much the unsuspecting and kind-hearted Grays were hurt by it.

Meanwhile Thomson was getting into print. He found time amid the exacting routine of his teaching to write his first essay on Shelley, and it was printed in the *National Reformer*. The latter magazine was founded this very year by Charles Bradlaugh, an old friend of the poet's, who was destined to be one of his most influential friends during the remainder of his life. Thomson had first met Bradlaugh when the latter was a private soldier at Ballincollig, and they had read and talked much together there. There is a story that during summer evenings Thomson used to walk up and down with Bradlaugh while the latter was on picket duty, discussing society, politics and religion. Bradlaugh had been from their first acquaintance a radical in politics, and, with the *National Reformer* as an organ, soon made his name unmentionable to English ears polite. He was impulsive and generous, with all the positiveness of opinion and boundless ambition of the reformer. Mr. Dobell in his memoir of Thomson regretted, not without justice, that

Bradlaugh was an Englishman rather than an American. Bradlaugh's reputation in England can be understood when it is realized that he was already urging control of births, and some of the more advanced views of the modern eugenists, upon Mid-Victorian England. He was likewise an honest zealot in the cause of a more democratic government, and not at all orthodox in his religious creed. In the two latter directions he was destined to exert considerable influence on the more hesitating and uncertain genius of Thomson. Bradlaugh had corresponded with the poet ever since their separation in Ireland in 1853, and on the organization of the *National Reformer,* he urged Thomson to contribute to it. During the next fifteen years his old friend printed in it his critical essays, and some of his finest poems. One of the first poems contributed was the *Dead Year,* a darkly powerful lyric allegory which sums up the events of the year 1860, after the fashion of Dryden's *Annus Mirabilis.* Despite the poet's approval of the democratic upheaval in Italy, whereon he sets the poetic blessing of Dante and Shelley, nevertheless he finds the world sad and filled with gloomy, purposeless slaughter. The "confirmation of the old despair" had now grown into a stern, biting utterance of the wrongs of the world.

Thomson's poetic tribute to Shelley, who had proved the strongest influence on the early years

of his own artistic development, was written in
the next year. Thomson's view of the "poet of
poets" is expressed in an allegorical narrative
poem much akin in spirit to Matthew Arnold's
more famous prose description of the "beautiful
and ineffectual angel, beating in the void his
luminous wings in vain." Thomson's *Shelley* is
written in the seven-line Chaucerian stanza of
which the latter poet is said to have been fond.
Thomson's great love for Shelley is due to the
obvious similarities of their opinions. Both were
radicals in politics and creeds, both celebrated
love in passionate poetry of a symbolic nature,
both were idealists and grew sad that the real
world should differ so vastly from the world of
their imagination. Yet the disciple lacks that
noble though questionable philosophy of sin, and
that glowing vision of the glories of the future
world.

Thomson also paid his tribute to Elizabeth
Barrett Browning, who died in 1861. He had
long been an admirer of her poems, as is seen
from his letters from Ireland to Agnes Gray in
the fifties. His fine eulogy of the dead poetess
concludes:

"Keats and Shelley sleep at Rome,
　　She in well-loved Tuscan earth;
Finding all their death's long home
　　Far from their old home of birth.

[ 53 ]

Italy, you hold in trust
Very sacred English dust."

But although only three poems have survived
from 1861, the last, *To Our Ladies of Death,* is
one of Thomson's greatest and most characteristic poems. His prayer for oblivion had been
uttered before in *Mater Tenebrarum,* but with a
more restless and uncertain anguish. In the
*Ladies of Death* the passion is more pure, and
the style is more direct, and more majestically
powerful. There are no doubts or expectations
here, but a calm acceptance of natural laws. The
holy Lady of Beatitudes, who represents individ-
ual and conscious immortality, and the horrible
Lady of Annihilation, who represents eternal
death, in turn appear before the poet but fail to
solace him. Last comes the Lady of Oblivion,
the spirit of peaceful fusion into the world-spirit.
Of her he says:

"Thou hauntest twilight regions, and the
    trance
    Of moonless nights when stars are few
        and wan
Within black woods; or over the expanse
    Of desert seas abysmal; or upon
Old solitary shores whose populous graves
Are rocked in rest by ever-moaning waves,
Or through vast ruined cities still and lone.

[ 54 ]

"The weak, the weary, and the desolate,
   The poor, the mean, the outcast, the
      opprest,
All trodden down beneath the march of
      Fate,
   Thou gatherest, loving Sister, to thy
      breast.
Soothing their pain and weariness asleep,
There in thy hidden Dreamland hushed and
      deep
Dost lay them, shrouded in eternal rest."

The poet realizes the eternal interchange of
matter, and knows that in his corporeal sub-
stance he will again enter into living things. Yet
his prayer for himself, like Shakespeare's great
sonnet, "Tired with all these, for restful death I
cry," is for the peaceful oblivion which only death
can bestow upon him:

"Weary of living isolated life,
   Weary of hoping hopes for-ever vain,
Weary of struggling in all-sterile strife,
   Weary of thought which maketh nothing
      plain,
I close my eyes and hush my panting breath,
And yearn for Thee, divinely tranquil
      Death
To come and soothe away my bitter pain."

In more ways than one, this great poem points forward with sombre insistence to the *City of Dreadful Night*. The peculiarly effective stanza form in which it and the later *City* are written, was, as Thomson himself afterwards confessed, taken from Browning's *Guardian Angel,* it is an ironic fact that the most optimistic English poet should thus provide for the most pessimistic of English poets a vehicle for the most pessimistic poem in the English language. It is noteworthy that in Browning's poem the fifth and sixth lines end with a feminine couplet. Thomson in the *Ladies of Death* made this couplet a masculine rhyme. Later in the *City of Dreadful Night* he restored the feminine couplet as he had found it in Browning. That the stanza of the *Ladies of Death* is not as effective as that of the *Guardian Angel* or the *City,* is quite obvious. In the latter poems the feminine couplet produces a passionate unrest, a hovering uncertainty, which the masculine last line solves, closing the stanza with firmness and power.

Thomson had taught in the army for ten years when his connection with teaching was severed forever. This change took place in October, 1862, and it marks with no little clearness the end of an epoch in his life. There seems to be some doubt as to the exact circumstances of the poet's dismissal from the army, and certain critics and

[ 56 ]

reviewers have questioned, but apparently without justification, Mr. Salt's account of the affair:

"In 1862, when his regiment was at Portsmouth, it chanced that Thomson went on a visit to a fellow schoolmaster at Aldershot, and in the course of a stroll in the neighborhood of the camp, one of the party, out of bravado or for a wager, swam out to a boat which was moored on a pond where bathing was prohibited. An officer demanded the names of those present, and on this being refused, further altercation followed, with the result that a court-martial was held on the recalcitrant schoolmasters. No real blame seems to have been attached to Thomson, but he paid the penalty of being one of the incriminated party, and was discharged from the service on October 30, 1862."

Thomson's first dated poem, *Love's Dawn*, had been written in 1852. His last poem written while still a teacher was the *Ladies of Death*, in 1862. In these ten years he had served his apprenticeship to verse, and his last poem shows his powers almost matured, and his technique almost perfected. Except for the *Ladies of Death*, none of these poems would have survived had his poetic career terminated here. On the whole, Thomson's life in the army was probably an advantage to him. He had been long stationed in the country, and his later poems attest a keen acquaintance with nature by their striking metaphors and unexpectedly graphic details. Had he gained all his imagery from books, he could never have written the *City of Dreadful Night*. On the other hand, the loose, rough camp life no doubt developed his craving for alcohol, which cast so sinister a shadow over his later years. It also accustomed him to roughing it alone, and did much to develop the Bohemianism latent in his temperament.

# CHAPTER IV

## HACKWORK IN LONDON (1862-1870)

THOMSON'S dismissal from the army was so sudden that he was left in doubt how he would make his living. He naturally thought of hack-writing, but wished to procure some other employment that would tide him over immediate expenses until that notoriously ill-paid occupation should prove a sufficient source of income. Bradlaugh, to whose *National Reformer* Thomson had contributed for several years, at once got the poet a position in the office of a London solicitor, of which he was the manager, opened the columns of his paper to him, and took him into his own home in Tottenham, where Thomson remained for the next four years. Bradlaugh's young daughters, Alice and Hypatia, were very fond of the poet, as indeed most children seem to have been all through his life. He took them to the theatre, told them fairy stories, and romped with them. Outwardly he seemed a not too successful but cheery and likable clerk and literary hack. This stay at the Bradlaughs' proved one of the happiest periods in his life, yet there is always the shadow of the old melancholy and the unforgettable sorrow mingled with it.

It was unfortunate for Thomson that his poetry should appear so exclusively in the *National Reformer*. Bradlaugh's paper seemed far from respectable to the upper classes of Mid-Victorian society, and was for the most part read by laboring men. Consequently Bradlaugh's own articles, written in a fine, slashing, controversial style, quite obscured the poems by his friend, B. V., which from time to time were included with them. Thomson himself was too much the poet and dreamer, and too little the cocksure, assertive reformer, to do popular poetry or prose for such an audience. Says Mr. Salt of his position:

"His part, however, was more that of a free-lance than that of a recognized leader; for his intense individuality, coupled with his almost cynical disbelief in the possibility of any human progress, must always have prevented his giving himself heart and soul to a 'cause.' He worked, as he himself avowed, on the side of liberty and free thought, not because he believed in the ultimate triumph of these principles, but simply because he was prompted thereto by a natural instinct and inclination. His hatred of all fuss and sham, and his impatience of the occasional 'clap-trap' and false sentiment not wholly sepa-

rable from any popular movement, made him
at times a sarcastic critic of his own party
no less than of his adversaries."

Yet the poet would have found it almost impossible to publish his fearless and fiery verses else-
where. "For me," Thomson once remarked in a
letter in reference to the *National Reformer,* "its
supreme merit consists in the fact that I can say
in it what I like how I like; and I know not
another periodical in Britain which would grant
me the same liberty or license." With Bradlaugh he had the most cordial relations, in spite
of the fact that the reformer never seemed to
realize the greatness of the poet, while the poet
was not always backward in jeering at the extrav-
agances of the reformer.

Like most men who take to hack-writing for
their living, Thomson became radical in his political views. To this end Bradlaugh also influenced
him considerably. This trend in the poet's interests is seen in two poems, the *Polish Insurgent* and
*Garibaldi Revisiting England,* written during his
stay at the Bradlaughs', and while the poet himself was secretary to the Polish Committee in
London. The former is a Browningesque and
quite impersonal study of the recklessly brave
Pole who leaves England, which he calls "Smith-
land," to fight the hopeless fight for his country.
In his poem on Garibaldi, Thomson shows that

love of Italy which he had perhaps caught from Shelley and Browning, and apostrophises her as

"Enceladus Italy, risen
   With earthquake, but pausing distrest
The left arm still brutally fettered
   And Peter's rock crushing the breast."

This sort of political verse now became a habit with Thomson which lasted till his death. Since they owed their production to the fact that he had become a hack-writer on current topics, they are consequently fine only in parts.

Between 1862 and 1866 Thomson wrote much prose. Some of it, such as *Bumble, Bumbledom, Bumblism,* an echo of Arnold's contemporary on-slaught on the Philistines, closely resembles the political poems already mentioned. Yet the *Lady of Sorrow,* the prose counterpart to the *City,* was also written during these years. Its sonorous periods, done in the imaginative style of De Quincey, cloak his old sorrow for Matilda Weller. Its three parts, the "Angel," the "Siren," and the "Shadow," reveal the supreme happiness he felt in her love, the dangerous temptations of life, and her abiding influence upon him which makes him dubious and melancholy in his later years. How-ever intense his rekindled affection for Helen Gray, it had quite burned out by now, and his first grief still possessed him.

Thomson wrote few poems between his coming to London and 1865. *The Three that shall be One* is an allegory of Love, who is betrothed to Death, yet seduced by Life and left on earth to comfort him. The tense and simple mysticism of this poem is quite rare in Thomson's poetry:

"Faint on the ground she lay;
 Love kissed the swoon away;
 Death then bent over her,
 Death the sweet comforter!
 Whispered with tearful smile
 'Wait but a little while,
 Then I will come to thee;
 We are one family.'"

*Ronald and Helen,* like the earlier *Tasso to Leonora* or *Bertram to Geraldine,* is an overlong love lament addressed to a dead mistress. Yet the form is new. Unlike his uniformly stanzaic poems of the fifties, this is a lyric medley much like Tennyson's *Maud.* Thomson was shortly to make more effective use of this medley form than in *Ronald and Helen,* which is uneven, confused and rather dull. But *The Fire that filled my heart of old,* written about the same time, is one of his richest and most vibrantly emotional lyrics, while *Vane's Story* (1864) is the most notable poem composed during his stay at the Bradlaughs'.

After Thomson left the army school and took

[ 63 ]

up writing in London, much conventionality in thought and style departed from his verse, and the present poem is less florid and ornate than his earlier work. *Vane's Story* is an account of the poet's vision of his lost love, Matilda, told in the imaginative and fantastically irregular manner of Browning's *Christmas Eve* and *Easter Day*. The poet dreams that he is visited by "Her, the Rose of Heaven," somewhat as before in the *Deliverer*. She chides him for failing to gain fame as a poet, and grieves over his doubts of a future life. The poem is a curious mixture of supernatural and commonplace realism, of spirituality and impudent sneers at religion, of nervous comic mockery and the sincere confessions of a victim of insomnia and melancholia. Some critics have objected to this blending of seriousness and mockery, as they have to that in Browning's more famous poems. Not a few have been shocked and offended at the poet's flippant religious speculations, and at the Heaven which he terms a "bland Beau monde." In this respect, indeed, the iron of Calvinism had entered his soul, and when he reacted, he did so fearlessly and without compromise:

> "Then I give God my scorn and hate,
> And turning back from Heaven's gate
> (Suppose me got there!) bow, *Adieu!*
> *Almighty Devil, damn me too!*"

The Mid-Victorians were not noted for their nice perception of the ridiculous, especially in matters of Christian belief. Their feeling toward such thrusts as this can easily be imagined. Yet *Vane's Story*, apart from its close autobiographical truth, contains some passages of an almost Shelleyan melody:

> "There was a Fountain long ago,
>  A fountain of perpetual flow,
>  Whose purest springlets had their birth
>  Deep in the bosom of the earth.
>  Its joyous wavering silvery shaft
>  To all the beams of morning laughed,
>  Its steadfast murmurous crystal column
>  Was loved by all the moonbeams solemn;
>  From morn to eve it fell again
>  A singing many-jeweled rain,
>  From eve to morn it charmed the hours
>  With whispering dew and diamond show-
>      ers;
>  Crowned many a day with sunbows bright,
>  With moonbeams halo'd many a night;
>  And so kept full its marble urn,
>  All fringed with fronds of greenest fern,
>  O'er which with timeless love intent
>  A pure white marble goddess leant:"

Despite its carelessness of diction, its indifference to all the established literary canons, and the levity of the theological footnotes scattered through it, *Vane's Story* is one of the half dozen greatest poems Thomson ever wrote.

The year 1865, the last that Thomson spent with the Bradlaughs', marks the high point of cheerfulness in his poetry. The poet's considerable sense of humor temporarily allowed him to enjoy those incongruities in life which tortured him so greatly during his darker hours. In a short poem, *Art,* Thomson utters a rather cynical conclusion concerning the relation of art to life:

"Singing is sweet; but be sure of this,
　Lips only sing when they cannot kiss.

　　*　　　*　　　*　　　*　　　*

"Had she let his arm steal round her waist
　Would the lovely portrait yet be traced?

"Since he could not embrace it flushed and
　　　warm
　He has carved in stone the perfect form.

"Who gives the fine report of the feast?
　He who got none and enjoyed it least."

While Thomson realized that in his poetry he had always open an escape from the burdens of life which were sometimes almost unsupportable, yet he had no illusions about art for art's sake. This poem was an especial favorite with George

Meredith, as that poet and novelist declared in a very cordial letter to Thomson.

But the best poem of this year, *Sunday up the River,* is the most light-hearted work he ever produced, and eventually attracted the attention of Froude and Kingsley. Like *Ronald and Helen,* it is a lyric medley which narrates a rambling story of holiday love up the Thames. There is a keen good humor in the poet's enthusiastic assertion that

"I love all hearty exercise
  That makes one strain and quiver,
And best of all I love and prize
  This boating on the river."

which is shortly followed by the very human reflection,

"How sinful *any* work to do
  In this Italian weather"

and finally the confession that

"Our skiff beneath the willow lies
  Half stranded and half floating."

After his description of the beauties of nature,

"The sky was pale with fervor,
  The distant trees were grey,
The hill-lines drawn like waves of dawn
  Dissolving in the day,"

his ironical amusement at the holiday maker's
outrageous plebeian appearance is equally delightful,

> "My shirt is of the soft red wool,
>    My cap is azure braided
> By two white hands so beautiful
>    My tie mauve-purple shaded."

In a concluding passage which has been moral-
ized over vastly too much, the hero produces a
"pocket-pistol" of "Jameson's Irish Whiskey,"
and the poem ends with a genial and happy-
hearted panegyric of life and love.  There is no
clearer example in all Thomson's poetry of his
whimsical and charming good fellowship than
here.

In an equally cheerful vein, though less sustained in lyrical power, is its sister medley, *Sunday at Hampstead* (*an idle idyll by a very
humble member of the great and noble London
mob*).  Thomson is not at all ashamed of his
Bohemianism, yet he is rarely over-ostentatious
about it.  In the pursuits of the vulgar he takes
a huge relish:

> "We can laugh out loud when merry,
>    We can romp at kiss-in-the-ring,
>    We can take our beer at a public,
>    We can loll on the grass and sing.

*     *     *     *     *

"Mary and Dick so grandly
  Parade suburban streets;
  His waistcoat and her bonnet
  Proving the best of treats.

"Mary is going to chapel
  And what takes her there, do you guess?
  Her sweet little duck of a bonnet
  And her new second-hand silk dress."

Yet along with the realistic good humor, there are
here, as in *Sunday up the River,* rapturous and
beautiful love lyrics:

"Day after day of this azure May
  The blood of the Spring has swelled in my
          veins,
  Night after night of broad moonlight
  A mystical dream has dazzled my brains."

Thomson himself is, of course, "Lazy," the hero
of the poem, and laughs heartily at himself. On
the whole, these two gay and good-humored
poems have a sweetness, richness and simplicity
about them almost unique among Victorian poetry
of the medley type, yet they are not at all alien to
the temperament of the author of the *City of
Dreadful Night.* As that is the consummate
expression of the dark side of his life, so they
are the fullest expression of his sunnier moments.
No optimist could be so rapturous had he not also

known the pangs of sorrow, nor could a pessimist who was not also partially an idealist be so vividly and poignantly despairing. Here the scale inclines to cheerfulness and love, yet shortly we shall see it sink to the "confirmation of the old despair." The minor poems of this year, *Shameless,* a scene in Kew, and *Low Life,* a dialogue between two lovers in a train, are cheerful and obviously inspired by Browning. *Polycrates on Waterloo Bridge* is a rather amusing hack-satire.

In 1866 Thomson left the Bradlaugh home in Tottenham to live as a "single man" lodger, as Mr. Dobell puts it, for the rest of his life. He still remained on intimate and even affectionate terms with the Bradlaughs, however, and most of the scanty knowledge we have of his whereabouts and occupations are derived from letters subsequently written to Hypatia or Alice Bradlaugh. The change was in every way unfortunate for the poet, as it secluded him from cheerful company, and aggravated his melancholia by the solitude which it imposed. In *Philosophy,* written about this time, the poet invokes the beautiful shams of life, and resolves not to probe too curiously into the truth:

> "If Midge will pine and curse its hours away
> Because Midge is not Everything For-aye,
> Poor Midge thus loses its one summer day,
> Loses its all—and winneth what, I pray?"

In *Life's Hebe* he is more resolute, though less subtle. This poem is an allegory of life. Hebe offers her cup to all men in youth, but none will take it as she gives it. Yet if its contents are diluted with wine or honey they become poisonous. The natural man escapes by mixing them with water. Only the poet drinks the contents unmixed, and it is found that he returns the cup fuller than when he received it. The moral is, that if one is to enjoy life, he must embrace it boldly and without hesitation.

Thomson's next significant poem, *L'ancien Régime,* was written in 1867. Again we see his radical political tendencies, for he vigorously satirizes the monarchical government of England. His views are presented even more clearly in his prose essay, *Proposals for the Speedy Extinction of Evil and Misery,* which about this time was inspired by Swift and written with a certain amount of his power. Thomson, unlike his beloved Shelley, did not believe in the perfectability of mankind. Toward almost all philanthropic ventures he was gloomy and sceptical. He thought that "all proselytism is useless and absurd." In *Indolence—a Moral Essay* he declares that, "In our time and country we have a plague of busy-bodyism, certainly more annoying and perhaps more noxious than the plague of idleness. One comes across many earnest and energetic characters who are no longer men, but simply

machines for working out their missions." The
wonder of it was that Thomson could, with such
views as these, continue to hold the friendship of
the fiery and uncompromising Bradlaugh.

From what can be learned of the poet's life at
this time, it seems that he was too busy to write
much poetry, and did only hack prose articles on
political topics. The *Naked Goddess* of 1867 is,
however, a significant poem. It is an allegorical
story of the untameable Goddess of Nature,
whom the city-folk vainly attempt to cloak in
robes of piety or science. She refuses to conform
to the laws of the arch-priest or the sage, and
bestows her blessing only on the little children
who can understand her and are willing to follow
her. The *Two Lovers* swiftly and vigorously
narrates an Oriental tale of love and the mockery
of Fate. But Thomson's greatest poem since
*Sunday up the River* is the powerful and very
original *In the Room,* one of the greatest poems
he ever wrote. Thomson had now been in solitary lodgings in Pimlico for two years, first in
Denbigh Street and then in what is now Warwick
Street. A few years before he had written feel-
ingly of William Blake:

"There were thousands and thousands of
     human kind
  In this desert of brick and stone;
But some were deaf and some were blind
  And he was there alone."

[ 72 ]

*In the Room* concentrates all the loneliness of a great city within a single dingy lodging-room. This room had once been glorified by love, but its beautiful mistress had departed, and its present master grown morose, has committed suicide and is lying dead on the bed. In turn the furniture in the room tells the story of his increasing despair, his silent hours of morbid brooding, and his eventual death by poison:

"It lay, the lowest thing there, lulled
    Sweet-sleep-like in corruption's truce;
The form whose purpose was annulled,
    While all the other shapes meant use.
It lay, the *he* become now *it*,
    Unconscious of the deep disgrace,
Unanxious how its parts might flit
    Through what new forms in time and
        space.

"It lay and preached, as dumb things do,
    More powerfully than tongues can prate;
Though life be torture through and through,
    Man is but weak to plain of fate:
The drear path crawls on drearier still
    To wounded feet and hopeless breast?
Well, he can lie down when he will,
    And straight all ends in endless rest.

[ 73 ]

"And while the black night nothing saw,
    And till the cold moon came at last,
The old bed held the room in awe
    With tales of its experience vast.
It thrilled the gloom; it told such tales
    Of human sorrows and delights,
Of fever moans and infant wails,
    Of births and deaths and bridal nights."

When it is realized how personal a poet Thomson was, whether gay or sad, the reader can detect here the outcome of many bitter and lonely hours of despair, when suicide seemed to him a tempting escape. His old melancholy is again upon him, and he is one step nearer to the *City,* his masterpiece of despair. In fact, only one poem of note intervenes between the two, and that is *Weddah and Om-el-Bonain*. *Weddah,* written in 1868-69, is an Oriental love story in ottova rima, swiftly and powerfuly told. Unlike the ornate and melodiously digressive *Pot of Basil,* whose manner it nevertheless recalls, *Weddah* possesses a naked strength which Keats rarely if ever was master of. *Weddah* is the story of two lovers who are crushed by an omnipresent and all-powerful Fate. The whole poem has what Swinburne, who together with the Rossetti brothers greatly admired it, called a "forthright triumphant power," which Thomson had rarely revealed in his previous poems, and which we are destined to mark again in the *City of Dreadful Night*. Yet it was a characteristic bit of bad fortune that the poem was refused for *Fraser's Magazine* and left unprinted until the poet's second volume was collected.

The chief source of information concerning Thomson during this period of his life is his diary, which, despite his Bohemian habits, he regularly kept. Its most significant entry is for Sunday, November 4, 1869:

"Burned all my old papers, manuscripts and letters, save the book MSS. which have been already in great part printed. It took me five hours to burn them, guarding against chimney on fire, and keeping them thoroughly burning. I was sad and stupid— *scarcely looked into any;* had I begun reading them I might never have finished their destruction. All the letters; those I had kept for more than for twenty years; those I had kept for sixteen. I felt myself like one who, having climbed half-way up a long rope (thirty five on the 23rd inst.) cuts off all beneath his feet; he must climb on and can never touch the old earth again without a fatal fall. The memories treasured in the letters can never, at least in great part, be revived in my life again, nor in the lives of the friends yet living who wrote them. But after this terrible year I could do no less than consume the past. I can now better face the future, come in what guise it may."

What poems and what letters were destroyed in this fire can never be determined, and their loss must be regretted both by the poet's biographers and readers. Like many other poets of marked personality, Thomson is most himself in a minor poem. It is by no means impossible that the destruction extended to some poems of importance, as Thomson hardly glanced at what he burned. It is a plausible conjecture that among his letters were some written by Matilda, sixteen years before, as he differentiates between the letters kept for sixteen years, and those which he had received before 1853, the date of her death. The mood of gloomy and hopeless persistence is, however, increasingly characteristic both in his life and his writings. As a poet, he had served his apprenticeship; as a man, he had burned his bridges, and had come to living within the fading memories and dreams of his youth more and more completely.

## CHAPTER V

## TRAVELS AND *THE CITY* (1870-1874)

FOR the next four years of his life, Thomson devoted only a small portion of his time to literature, and was chiefly concerned with various mercantile and journalistic ventures, all of which failed with a unanimous promptness and completeness. Yet it was in the spare hours of these harassing years that the *City of Dreadful Night* grew gradually in his mind and on paper into its superbly powerful form. Roughly speaking, the first half of it was finished in 1870; the remaining portion after two years more of disappointment and melancholia in dingy London offices and lodgings. Like practically all his other poems, it is sincere and intensely personal, and until the background of his actual life during the period of its composition is realized, its merits cannot be fully appreciated.

Bradlaugh gave up business in London in 1870 or 1871, as Thomson says in a letter of 1872,

"in order to devote himself solely to the great business of illuminating the benighted intellect of the nation in social, political and religious matters. For some time after he left I did nothing, an occupation which would suit me extremely well, and for which I have fine natural talents that I have taken care to cultivate to the best of my abilities. That is, would suit me extremely well on a fortune, or in a semi-tropical climate; but here, without money, it is a luxury too ethereal for my taste. Afterwards, I did some work in a printing office, reading proofs, revising, etc.; and, as to this, I will only say that if ever you have the misfortune to be condemned to penal servitude, and they offer to commute the sentence for such work in a printing office, you had better stick to the penal servitude. I then became secretary *pro tem.* to one of the thousand companies which came into being last year, and in some very hard commercial campaigning have already had two companies killed under me. I am at present astride of a third, which may carry me out safely or may not; it has received two or three shot and sabre wounds already, but seems tough and tenacious of life. By-the-bye, our slain companies brought nobody down but the riders; our friendly foes, the share-holding public, having received all their money back. As I was nearly thirty when I came to London, I could not go through the regular course in any business, and have had to seize whatever honest chance offered. Perhaps some day I shall turn up a trump and win a good stake; it is much more probable that I shan't. In the meanwhile, having no one to look to but myself, I quietly take things as they come, and quietly let things go as they go, fortifying myself with that saying of the philosopher that it matters not whether in this vale of tears we wipe our eyes with a silk or a cotton handkerchief, or blink through tortoise-shell or gold-rimmed eye-glasses. Perhaps the said philosopher had himself the silk handkerchief and the gold-rimmed glasses, or perhaps he did not use a handkerchief or wear eye-glasses, and thus was able to be so philosophical on the subject. Not that I need to wipe my eyes in this vale of tears, for I always find the prospect much too sad or much too comical for weeping."

Thomson's various secretaryships, here so dismally yet good-temperedly referred to, were destined to cause him to cross the Atlantic. In the year 1872, when the above letter was written, he happened to be secretary of "The Champion Gold and Silver Mines Company," whose holdings were mostly in Central City, Colorado. Thither he was soon sent at the instigation of the directors of the company, to report to them upon the work which was being accomplished there, and to represent them upon the grounds. His account of the people and their customs, preserved in various letters to his friends, reminds the reader oddly of Mark Twain's "Roughing It" in its exaggerated and explosive humor.

"As to the drinking," Thomson wrote to a friend, "one anecdote will suffice. An officer sent out to cater for some divisions of the Army in the West, returned with six waggon-loads of whiskey and one of provisions. The commanding officer, having overhauled the stock, cried out, 'What the hell shall we do with all these provisions?' "

Thomson too was struck with the vastness and the undeveloped resources of America, and forgave the Americans much of their arrogance when he realized the tremendous causes of their sometimes vulgar enthusiasms. Himself a radical in politics, he could appreciate more completely than the typical English tourist, our internal "manifest destiny," and the fact that, as he put it,

"they are starting over here with all our experience and culture at their command, without any of the obsolete burdens and impediments which in the course of a thousand years have become inseparable from our institutions, and with a country which will want more labor and more people for many generations to come."

Thomson was likewise impressed with the wild Colorado mountain scenery during his eight months' stay at the mines, and in his later poems the reader can detect images remembered from his life in the West. His previous knowledge of nature had been gained for the most part in the lowlands of Ireland and southern England. Certain passages of the *City* written at this time perhaps, indicate the effect of the grandeur and vastness of the New World, as,

> "A trackless wilderness rolls north and
>       west,
> Savannahs, savage woods, enormous moun-
>       tains,
> Bleak uplands, black ravines with torrent
>       fountains. . . . "

Thus it came about that the *City* in its imagery was London, fringed with Colorado and seen at midnight. In his letters he had much to say of American scenery:

"This week we are to have a concert (in Central City), and also a lecture on the Darwinian Theory, admission one dollar. We have a theatre, and now and then a dance. The old, rough days with their perils and excitements, are quite over; the 'City' is civilized enough to be dull and commonplace, while not civilized enough to be sociable and pleasant. There are no beggars, and petty larceny is almost unknown; store keepers extort your money blandly and quietly, and the large larceny of selling mines at preposterous prices makes the people despise all larceny that is petty. . . .

"The hills surrounding us have been flayed of their grass and scalped of their timber, and they are scarred and gashed and ulcerated all over from past mining operations; so ferociously does little man scratch at the breasts of his great calm mother when he thinks that jewels are there hidden. . . .

"These foothills are distributed remarkably among the snowy ranges of mountains, curtain beyond curtain, fold beyond fold, twisting and heaving inextricably . . . one massy range ends in a promontory whose scarped and precipitous upper flanks gleam grand and savage, in their stony nakedness, like the gleaming of set white teeth in some swart Titanic barbarian. . . .

"From these higher hills one gets magnificent views. Vast billowy land seas, with dense woods and deep ravines and exquisitely emerald dells, whereon and whereover sleep and sweep immense shadows, and of all shades even at noonday, from bright green to solid black; beyond, a crescent of the mountains, some with broad fields or deep furrows of snow, some sheathed wholly with this white splendor; eastward toward the plains, what the eye cannot distinguish from a distant sea-line, faint or dark blue, level to the horizon, with pale streaks like the shadows of clouds and long shoals, and the haze of evaporation.

" . . . I have seen from here a terrible storm raging over the plains, dead-silent through remoteness: white lightnings momentarily surging up, veiling the stars, making the lower clouds ghastly, striking pale reflections from clouds at the zenith; and these broad sheets of white light were seamed and riven by intense darting lines of forked lightning, zig-zag, vertical, transverse, oblique."

But although the Colorado scenery improved his poems, the financial operations of its whilom exploiters did not benefit his pocket. By the end of 1872 the "Champion Gold and Silver Mines Co." disappeared in that hazy oblivion whither many similar ventures have both preceded and followed it. Thomson returned to London early in 1873, and for six months his pursuits are a mystery to his biographers. In July, 1873, owing to the efforts of his faithful friend, Bradlaugh, he became a war correspondent of the *New York World* in Spain, where the Carlist revolutionary movement was threatening the government. The ensuing campaign, however, was greatly disappointing to the newspaper world. The whole affair proved to be mainly a comic opera of alarms and excursions, and the only skirmishing Thomson saw was "more like a frolic of schoolboys than a serious fight." Owing to the grotesque refusal of the revolution to be spectacular, to a short attack of sunstroke, and no doubt to considerable personal indolence, he failed to provide sufficient copy for the *World* and was recalled early in the fall of '73, despite his just rejoinder that it was hardly his fault if the Spaniards refused to fight.

Several years afterwards Thomson wrote humorously of the trip and its consequences. When he first returned to London, however, there is no doubt that he was profoundly discouraged. Moreover, the sudden return from a tropical summer to a damp autumn in London affected his health, and for weeks, as Mr. Salt tells us, he could not read, write or even smoke. His mind consequently turned back upon itself, and he again brooded over his continual failures against Fate. He was now nearing forty, and had no future to which he could look forward beside the regular routine of hackwork. His health and ambitions were declining, all his attempts in business had failed, and for over twenty years his poems and prose had been very poorly paid, and practically unnoticed. The haunting image of his dead love of twenty years ago tortured his mind with its increasing suggestion of what might have been, but its evanescent beauty could no longer console him in his dingy and monotonous existence in London. Religion had grown to be a hideous mockery and an impossible delusion. Neither was it good that he should be rooming alone in the unspeakable solitude of a great city. Before his despairing eyes, London rose shadowy through a dense and fateful gloom, with which the quavering yellow street-lamps strove in vain; a vast metropolis, whose sombre mansions concealed unthinkable wrongs and agonies beneath their shrouds of murky air; whose dreary streets were paced by wandering, hopeless ghosts, where groans were heard continually, and the muffled jar of unseen wheels. Over all hung a darkness which never was on land or sea. In scenes luridly vivid, like midnight lit up by lightning flashes, Thomson has described this "builded desolation," even to the "trackless wilderness" or "savannahs" and "savage woods" of Hampstead, where ten years before he had found such rapturous delight. Although love and life had failed him, one single consolation remained—the maturity of his poetic powers. The result is the *City of Dreadful Night,* the greatest single pessimistic poem in English, or perhaps in any literature.

Much criticism has been vapidly expended on the structure of this powerful and magnificent poem. It is divided into twenty-one sections, which regularly alternate the seven-line reflective stanza of the *Guardian Angel* and the *Ladies of Death,* and varying narrative stanzas of three, four and six lines. In the latter narrative cantos, which of course include all the even sections, the poet's wanderings through the city are related, while in the more lyrical and massive odd cantos, he reflects upon what he hears and sees there. This alternation of form and variation of lyrical and narrative treatment relieves what would otherwise be a tremendous monotony in its constant burden of despair.

Here, as always, Thomson is an intensely personal poet, and it is because of this fact that the *City* is a great poem. To an intellectual sceptic and pessimist like Arnold, even his own personality seemed to him too petty to become the source of a dark outlook on the universe. Arnold could, despite the Greek maxim that "Man is the measure of all things," disregard the limitations of the world which his own nature compelled him to see, and view the universe objectively and impersonally as all mankind must always see it. But Thomson, lacking Arnold's education in the "grand style" of Greek poetry, and his breadth of outlook as an Oxford graduate born into an intellectual heritage, felt himself a pessimist more on account of his own sorrow than because of the inherent sadness of the universe. Hence the latter poet found within his own personality, in his own hopes and fears, his dreams and disillusionments, the inspiration for this greatest of his poems.

In the Proem to the *City* he declares that he has no wish to disturb the happiness of others, but that at times "a cold rage seizes him" to show Truth in all her ancient ugliness. Much akin to Tennyson's "sad, mechanic exercise Like dull narcotics, numbing pain," is his confession of his satisfaction in writing poetry:

"Because it gives some sense of power and
        passion
In helpless impotence to try to fashion
Our woe in living words, howe'er uncouth."

Thomson realized better than any of his critics that his city is built in a sleepless nightmare, and that in the clear daylight it "dissolveth like a dream of night away." Yet he declares that if such a dream returns night after night, and year after year, it cannot be distinguished from life itself, which is composed essentially of habitual dreams, whose reality is measured only by the frequency and force of their recurrence. Hence, his city has none of the conventional and outworn imagery of the ruined city beloved of romantic poets, but consists of orderly streets and spacious mansions. It is London itself, seen in a moment of despair, and described with a lurid force unequalled since Coleridge and De Quincey.

It is a subjective city, confessedly, but supremely real to Thomson. Amid

> "The soundless solitudes immense
> Of ranged mansions dark and still as
> tombs"

there are other inhabitants too, with "worn faces that look deaf and blind Like tragic masks of stone." With such fiercely vivid Dantean phrases he paints the hopeless woes of all who have entered this "città dolente." All the sorrows of humanity are found here, and the poet's hand at times grows a little weary of recording them. First he meets a weary pilgrim who, as a victim of Fate, can only bemoan "Dead Faith, dead Love, dead Hope." Faith could not overcome the graveyard, Hope perished through poverty and bitter adversity in a hovel, and Love died in a villa through sensuality, bringing false suspicions and murder in its train. Thomson too held that "All men kill the thing they love." A second victim of Love and Fate he meets, who declaims one of the poet's greatest lyrics, "As I came through the desert, . . ." This man, who is of course Thomson himself, had lost his love and his hope, and consequently feared nothing, even the horrors of nature. But his love comes to him with a lamp which is her own bleeding heart. She vainly tries to wipe his brow clear of anguish. He feels himself two separate personalities, one his former self which swoons at her desolate beauty, the other his later self which watches it passive, and hopelessly endures without a sign all the tortures which Fate can inflict. The spectre vanishes on the tide with the corpse of his former self, his memories of love long years ago, while the other soulless and impotent self cries out with the simplicity of the Greek tragedies,

"They love, their doom is drear,
   Yet they nor hope nor fear;
   *But I, what do I here?*"

There is another weird scene at the gate of the city, where all the weary pilgrims who would enter must obey Dante's stern mandate, "Lasciate ogni speranza, voi ch'entrate." Some, who have no hopes to abandon at the gate, are denied entrance, and suffer in a torpid Limbo without. Inside the city, ghosts of former men walk the streets in despair. The poet overhears the conversation of two outworn sufferers. They are atheists, since they cannot believe in the fiendlike God who must have created such a world. To these men, religion is a bitter "rhapsody of words":

"As if a Being, God or Fiend could reign,
At once so wicked, foolish and insane,
As to produce men when he could refrain!"

This is a far cry from the Irvingites. The poet continues in harsh and powerful stanzas:

"The world rolls round for-ever like a mill;
It grinds out death and life and good and ill;
It has no purpose, heart or mind or will.

"While air of Space and Time's full river flow,
The mill must blindly whirl unresting so:
It may be wearing out, but who can know?

"Man might know one thing were his sight less dim;
That it whirls not to suit his petty whim,
That it is quite indifferent to him.

"Nay, does it treat him harshly as he saith?
It grinds him some slow years of bitter breath,
Then grinds him back into eternal death."

The next narrative episode is a powerful and pathetically beautiful tribute to his lost love.   In a fine mansion a lover is praying beside his dead mistress:

> "The chambers of the mansion of my heart,
>   In every one wherein thine image dwells,
>   Are black with grief eternal for thy sake.

> \*        \*        \*        \*        \*

> "I kneel here patient as thou liest there;
>   As patient as a statue carved in stone,
>   Of adoration and eternal grief.

> \*        \*        \*        \*        \*

> "While thou dost not awake I cannot move;
>   And something tells me thou wilt never
>       wake,
>   And I alive feel turning into stone."

As the poet glides silently from the mansion, he reflects that,

> "This was the festival that filled with light
>   That palace in the City of the Night."

Then the poet wanders into a vast, dark cathedral, where a doom-stricken congregation listens to the despairing sermon delivered in a "voice of solemn stress."   To this sombre refuge have all manner of men come, the defeated reformer, the victim of drugs, the professional comedian, the ecstatic ascetic, the able ruler, the evangelist, the voluptuary, the artist and the hero. Nor is there any joy because of their community of sorrow. All stand apart, and cannot bridge the chasms between self and self. Doom, and not their environment, has made them forever sorrowful.

The preacher finds, like Tennyson in *In Memoriam,* that Evolution is a bitter thing for mankind, which has no "special clause" for man, but which is only the method that Fate has chosen to impel change through the universe:

> "If toads and vultures are obscene to sight,
>   If tigers burn with beauty and with might,
>     Is it by favor, or by wrath of Fate?
>
> "All substance lives and struggles evermore
>   Through countless shapes continually at
>       war,
>     By countless interactions interknit:
>
> "If one is born a certain day on earth,
>   All times and forces tended to that birth,
>     Not all the world could change or hinder
>       it."

He concludes that if man would not fulfill his poor life, which Fate has ordered and over which he has no control, that he is at least free to end it when he will "without the fear of waking after death." He finds a tragic irony in the fact that man's one short life should be a spasm of pain between two eternal oblivions.

In a tangled, poisonous copse the poet next meets a dotard who crawls painfully backward, in an endeavor to regain the innocence and delight of a previous existence. Yet the way is dark and he has unknowingly traversed all its winding paths over and over again. Thomson had been fascinated by the Oriental idea of the transmigration of souls, as we have seen in the *Ladies of Death,* but here he finds it to be only another tragic mockery of existence. At length he comes to the dark River of Suicides, and overhears two weary men discuss self-murder as a means of escaping from life. Here Thomson's own reasons for avoiding the escape which he had pictured with such ghastly distinctness in *In the Room,* are made clear. He wishes to see "what shifts are yet in the dull play," and to "refrain from grieving Dear foolish friends by our untimely leaving." Yet with admirable courage he concludes that "it is but for one night after all," and that even Fate cannot at length deny to him and to all men "That one best sleep that never wakes again."

The *City* embodies a typical, frequent and perhaps dominant mood in the poet's life. He well knows that on some mornings the inhabitants

[ 93 ]

of the "dolent city" awake as though reborn, and freed for a time from its grasp. Yet this always proves only a mocking reprieve, never a triumphant escape. Once that city's terrible streets have been trod, hope withers and the victim is helpless under the doom of his terrible dreams. Time is an intolerable burden to him, and only in the annihilation of death is there any peace. That some men are free from the "city's curse" only intensifies his pain, and there is no saving community of sorrow within its walls. Over the city the stars burn on, night after weary night, more lasting but not eternal symbols of the meaningless chaos which pervades all the cosmos.

The *City* ends with two tremendous allegories. In the first, a triumphant angel in stone opposes the vacant-eyed Sphinx of Nature. In turn the angel's wings and sword fall, and it becomes a doomed and helpless man. Then the man falls, while there remains only the "cold majestic face" of the eternal Sphinx, "whose vision seemed of infinite void space." In the second and concluding allegory, Thomson brilliantly describes Melancholia, the patron saint of the *City*. He has transferred the actual details and the strange fascination of Dürer's great engraving into poetry. She is the emblem of the human race, which struggles with a vain but continual heroism against its bitter destiny. She knows that in the end all struggles are frustrated, that

"None can pierce the vast black veil uncertain
Because there is no light beyond the curtain,
That all is vanity and nothingness."

So she rests there forever in "bronze sublimity"
over her tragic city, a symbol of the poet's own
sad, unshaken heroism in the face of certain
disaster:

"The moving moon and stars from east to
west
Circle before her in the sea of air;
Shadows and gleams glide round her solemn
rest.
Her subjects often gaze up to her there;
The strong to drink new strength of iron
endurance;
The weak, new terrors; all, renewed assur-
ance
And confirmation of the old despair."

Thus ends the *City of Dreadful Night,* one of the
saddest and most terrible poems any man ever
wrote.

Thomson finished the *City* in 1874 during
intervals between various hackwork—economic
and political articles, educational and literary
essays, and many other of the sorry affairs that

the present pays for and the future forgets. He
had again taken up fairly regular contributing to
Bradlaugh's *National Reformer* and it was in this
dubiously respectable but open-minded magazine
that the *City* was first published in four install-
ments, from March 22 to May 17, 1874. From
this time dates what recognition Thomson ever
received as a poet.

A few leading reviews paid their acknowledg-
ments, mostly, despite Mr. Dobell's enthusiastic
account of the matter, with no little air of patron-
age. The *City,* like all his previous articles and
poems, had been signed "B. V." and his anonymity, though quite characteristic of his apparent
indifference to public opinion, hindered his becom-
ing as well known as he might otherwise have
been. Yet to a poet discouraged by twenty years
of obscurity, it was no small pleasure to receive
recognition from many other noted literary men
and women. George Meredith, P. B. Marston,
the blind poet, W. M. Rossetti, and Saintsbury
were at once attracted by the obvious merits of
the *City*. George Eliot congratulated him in a
stately but sincere letter on his "distinct vision
and grand utterance." Bertram Dobell tells with
a pardonable wealth of detail how he found out
who "B. V." was from the *National Reformer,*
and became an intimate friend of the poet. Even
in America, both Emerson and Longfellow recognized the greatness of the *City*.

# CHAPTER VI

## THE "SEVEN SONGLESS YEARS"
### (1874-1881)

TO say that the sudden recognition accorded the *City of Dreadful Night* by such a distinguished company of authors and critics did not influence Thomson's later years, would be obviously untrue. Yet the tragic struggle of his inner life seems to have been changed very little by it. His poetic energies had for a time almost burned themselves out in the *City*. What Thomson called his "seven songless years" ensued when, for the first time in his life, good poems from his hand would probably have attracted general attention, and won him fame with the general public, instead of the limited circle of critics who already knew his work. Between 1874 and 1881 he wrote mostly hack-verse for distinctly secular purposes, such as the *Prologue to the Pilgrimage of Saint Nicotine of the Holy Herb,* which is perhaps as good advertising verse as the average major poet can write. A few satirical poems also can occasionally be found, which have the form and some of the humorous zest of

Browning. Usually these drift into religious or theological channels, and are hardly orthodox. *Bill Jones on Prayer,* while a hastily written *jeu d'esprit,* illustrates Thomson's position rather well:

"God helpeth him who helps himself,
  They preach to us as a fact,
Which seems to lay up God on the shelf,
  And leave the man to act.
Which seems to mean—You do the work,
  Have all the trouble and pains,
While God, that Indolent Grand Old Turk,
  Gets credit for the gains."

These years, however, bulk large in his critical prose works, and some imaginative pieces, like *In our Forest of the Past* and *Saint Sylvester's Day,* are occasionally found among them. Almost all the work that he did during these seven years bespeaks industry, but little of that passionate imaginative power which his greatest writing reveals. He vainly tried for several years to find a publisher for his poems, but more through his financial needs than through ambition. He came more and more to live within his own mind, with even more torpor and indifference than before. In spite of his hard grasp of fact, he often failed to distinguish the real world from that inner and imaginary world into which he retired more and more as the years went by. Mr. Salt records a curious instance of this trait from the poet's diary:

> "*Sunday, March 2*—Queer dream, morng. Condemned to death for sort of manslaughter on one who deserved it for wronging another. No remorse, no fear, some perplexity as to chance of commut. to imprisonment for life. Some trouble on waking to make sure it had been a dream."

Thomson supported himself in his lonely lodgings entirely by his hackwork. He was a confirmed smoker, and was increasingly given to fits of intemperance when his melancholia, rendered now more acute by his growing insomnia, proved too unbearable. His intemperance was periodic, like a disease. G. W. Foote, an intimate friend, wrote of this infirmity:

> "He was not a toper; on the contrary, he was a remarkably temperate man, both in eating and drinking. His intemperate fits came on periodically, like other forms of madness; and naturally as he grew older and weaker they lasted longer, and the lucid intervals became shorter. The fits were invariably preceded by several days of melancholy, which deepened and deepened until it became intolerable. Then he flew to the alcohol, so naturally and unconsciously that

when he returned to sanity he could seldom
remember the circumstances of his collapse."

Other intimate friends of the poet during the
"seven songless years" have borne testimony to
the grim, soldierly courage with which Thomson
fought off these attacks. All seem to agree that
during this period of his life they recurred several months apart. It may be that he sometimes
took opium, although certainly never to the extent
that some moralists would have us believe.

Thomson's diary for 1875 has unfortunately
been lost, and the chief source of information
about the poet lies in his letters to Bertram
Dobell. While these deal mainly with Thomson's
vain efforts to find a publisher for his poems, yet
this correspondence also preserves the record of
his final separation from Bradlaugh, especially in
the following extracts:

"*January 18, 1875*—I'm still on the staff
of the noble N. R. but have been crowded
out of late. C. B. and Ajax (Mrs. Besant)
take up much room, and we wanted to bring
in other things. I'm always willing to give
way, especially when doing so saves me from
writing nonsense. I resume in next week's
number.

*April 17, 1875*—Your former note came
too late for me to let you know that I am

[ 100 ]

always late on Wednesdays.  On that night
the N. R. goes to press; I am not done with
it till about nine, Watts till about eleven; so
he and I with a few others generally spend
an hour or two together after nine, waiting
for the first proof.

*May 18, 1875*—You may tell anyone you
like my name, as the N. R. people and B.
haven't in the least respected the anonymity.
I shall put my name to the volume if published.  As to my position, I don't want
strangers to know that I am somewhat hard
up; it's none of their business.  They may
know that I help and contribute to the N. R.
for all I care. . . . Philip Bourke Marston
has been at the office wanting a copy of the
*City*.

*July 9, 1875*—I believe a good many
(copies of the prospective volume) would be
disposed of through advertisement in the
N. R.  I am quite off this now, B. having
taken the first opportunity of terminating
our connection, which I myself had only sub-
mitted to for some time past because it
afforded me mere subsistence.  So I must get
other engagements at once, and a published
volume would be of immense service to me.
Of course B. could not refuse my advertisement, nor do I suppose he would charge for
it even now, seeing that he had all the verses

[ 101 ]

for nothing; but I should send it to the office
in the ordinary way of business.

*August 24, 1875*—I go in for this new
paper (Foote and Holyoake's Secular
Weekly) thoroughly of course, not caring
to be gagged at the pleasure of Mr. B."

The facts concerning this permanent quarrel
which he had with Bradlaugh early in 1875, are
not clearly preserved. Dobell's Memoir is no
doubt quite just in laying the blame principally on
the poet. Since Thomson's dismissal from the
army, Bradlaugh had always been the poet's
greatest and most convenient aid. Bradlaugh had
housed him and procured for him a clerkship in
1862, had enabled him to print in the *National
Reformer* articles and poems which very few if
any magazines would accept, had got him his
position as war correspondent in Spain, and after
that failure had given him regular employment
on the *Reformer*. That by doing so Bradlaugh
did much to keep his own name alive, is the accident of fate rather than any intentional effort on
the poet's part. Bradlaugh was eminently practical, and largely insensitive to the poet's genius.
To him, Thomson was an intimate friend who
had made a failure of practical life. On the other
hand, the poet was usually very loyal in his friend-
ships, and just in his dealings with men. The real
wonder of it is, however, not that there should

have been a quarrel, but that the quarrel should have been so long delayed. Bradlaugh was a practical iconoclast, a man of action, and quite positive in his views. Thomson was at heart an idealist and a man of thought, who was interested in practical affairs only because he had to make a living. Had the rupture never taken place, perhaps the poet's last days might have proved less awful, for Thomson had come to lean upon the reformer's stronger and more positive nature in times of trouble, more than he himself realized at the time. Next perhaps to Matilda Weller, Bradlaugh exerted more influence upon Thomson's life than any other human being. The two men as a matter of fact had many common beliefs about religion and society, as Thomson had confessed some time before in a letter to his sister-in-law:

"So you are rather glad that I am no longer with B., exposed to the contagion of his dreadful heresies. To tell you the truth, I don't think that there's a pin to choose between his opinions as to things in general, and my own; only while he considers his opinions of the utmost importance, and is unwearied in the profitable task of converting the world to them, I care very little for mine, and don't believe the world capable of being benefited much by having any opinion whatever preached to it. But you must not blame him or anybody for my wicked opinions, which I have arrived at by the mere force of my own evil nature, influenced very little by the opinions of others. The Sunday school views of this life and dissolving views of a life hereafter proved quite unsatisfactory to this philosopher many years ago."

When the *National Reformer* was closed to him as a source of income, Thomson shifted to *Cope's Tobacco Plant,* a monthly published by Liverpool tobacco merchants. Although the purpose of this peculiar magazine was mainly to advertise the wares of its owners, yet it was not at all without literary pretensions. Thomson wrote critical essays for it upon Ben Jonson, Whitman, Hogg and Rabelais, as well as reviews on current literature, and hack articles on various phases of the tobacco business. To this paper he contributed until the end of his "seven songless years," when it was discontinued. His best critical work, however, such as his fairly well-known articles on Heine, were written for the *Secularist,* a short-lived radical journal to which his friend, G. W. Foote, gave him an entry. In this latter periodical Thomson printed articles on religion, society and literature, poems written during his earlier years, and took a vigorous if somewhat unwise part in the controversy which soon arose

between the *Secularist* and his old medium, the
*National Reformer*. It was in Foote's *Secularist* that he published his translations from Heine,
which drew a congratulatory letter from Karl
Marx, the noted economist and scholar. Heine
had influenced Thomson strongly in many of his
poems, notably in *Vane's Story*. The latter's
facility in translation is seen best, perhaps, in his
version of Heine's "Gods of Greece."

"I have never loved you, O ye Gods!
  For not at all to my mind are the Greeks,
  And the Romans I thoroughly hate;
  Yet pious compassion and sorrowful sym-
     pathy
    Possess my heart,
When I see you now above there
Desolate deities,
Dead, night-wandering shadows,
Frail clouds, driven by the wind,—
And when I think how mean and blatant
The Gods are who have overcome you,
The new, dominant, melancholy Gods,
So malignant in their sheep's clothing of
    humility—
O then seizes me a gloomy rage,
And I could shatter the new temple,
And fight for you, you ancient Gods,
For you and your joyous ambrosial sway,
And before your high altars

Broad-built and steaming with sacrifices,
I could even kneel and pray
And suppliant arms uplift.
Though always aforetime, O ye Gods,
In the battles and dissensions of men,
Ye have fought on the side of the strongest;
Yet man is more magnanimous than you,
And in the Battle of the Gods I range my-
    self
With the followers of the vanquished
    Gods!"

From 1876 until a month before his death,
Thomson lodged in 35 Alfred Street. His most
intimate friends, G. W. Foote of the *Secularist,*
with which paper the poet was at this time connected, and T. R. Wright, who had married the
widow of Thomson's old friend, Austin Holyoake, lived close at hand at 12 Gower Street.
As a consequence Thomson became almost a member of the Wright household during the last six
years of his life. His diary records the quiet and
uneventful evenings spent in the British Museum,
in his lodgings, or with these friends:

"*Wednesday, Jan. 8*—Bitter easterly.
Some sun. Morng & evng. Fair copy
*Memorial.* . . . Aftn, walk about Soho.
(Coal scuttle; after three years.) Moon
keen as crystal, sky pale and cloudless, stars

few and dim, ground like iron, wind like a razor.

*Monday, Feb. 17*—Fog morng. Some sun midday. Wet evg. Cool. N. W. Morng, up late, dawdled. (Poor strange cat in back coal-cellar and under kitchen since Saty. morng.) Aftn. Stroll Oxford St. also before dinner. Evng. Reading Erasme: *Elogie de la Folie* (Biblio. Nationale.) Slight bilious indigestion. listless and sleepy. Beer early for early bed.

*Ash Wednesday, Feb. 26*—Cold N. E. wind; glum; snow in the air, slight powder falling. Morng. to B. M. Shut. Did my Commination Service alone; cursing the idiots who close such a place on such a day. Stroll before dinner. Aftn, Gower St. Evg, writing bit of *Men of Letters*. Reading Goldsmith. Coals (1) full.

*Friday, Feb. 28*—The dull rheumatic pains shoulders and right arm continue; slight, but I rather fear after father.

*Thursday, Aug. 14*—Have got into a bad way of waking two or three hours before I want to get up (before 5 or 6) & being unable to sleep afterwards. Hence I arise weary at last; and am very drowsy after tea, when I want to read or write. This morng. awoke 5:40; this evg. had to lie down &

slept from 6:30 to 8:30; losing two good hours.

*Saturday, Nov. 8*—Athenæum, advt. of Egoist: cordial praise from Athenm, Pall Mall, Spectr, Examr. At length! At length! A man of wonderful genius & a splendid writer may hope to obtn. something like recogn. after working hard for thirty years, dating from his majority.

*Christmas Day*—Black fog midday, and until night. Morng. (late) answg Fraser's with receipt. Dined Gower St. Billiard & Evg. Home 12:20 or so. Bed past one.

*Wednesday, Dec. 31*—Saw Old Year out and New Year in at Mitchell's; with Wright's & Cards, Whist and Vingt-un."

Especially significant among these entries are the indications of the poet's failing health, which had been first seriously impaired on his Spanish trip in 1873, and had grown constantly worse from his sedentary life as a hack-writer in London. Insomnia is particularly mentioned in his diaries from 1873 to 1879. During the last year there were unmistakable signs of more serious disorders. He mentions "a queer catching pain" in the back, and a constriction "over and about the heart." As is evident from the entry in his diary for February 28 quoted above, he was apprehensive of a paralytic stroke like his father's forty years before.

Thomson's increasing weakness had the result of changing his pessimism from a frequent and vigorous emotional attitude, to a calm, settled intellectual conviction.  G. W. Foote (*Progress,* June, 1884) has sympathetically described the poet's feelings and beliefs at this period of his career:

"Thomson's life inclined him to a pessimistic view of nature, yet it must not be supposed that his philosophy was merely a matter of temperament.  He was little of a cynic and less of a misanthrope, and you could not have inferred his philosophy from his ordinary conversation.  He was naturally chary of talking about his ideas even to his intimate friends, but when he broke through his customary reticence he spoke with the quiet gravity of intense conviction. I well remember the first time he ever conversed with me on the subject.  It was a still summer's night, and we sat together on the Thames Embankment at Chelsea.  We smoked and chatted for a long time, and growing more communicative under the influence of that tender sunset, we gradually sank into the depths.  I found his pessimism as stubborn as adamant.  It was not a mood,

[ 109 ]

but a philosophy, the settled conviction of a keen spectator of the great drama of life. He admitted that he had no special reason to scorn his fellows; on the contrary, he had met many good friends, who had treated him 'better than he deserved.' But all that was beside the question. He denied the reality of progress in the world; there was revolution, but no forward movement; the balance of good and evil remained through all changes unchanged; and eventually the human race, with all its hopes and fears, its virtues and crimes, its triumphs and failures, would be swept into oblivion. In conclusion he quoted Shakespeare, a very rare thing with him; and he rose from his seat with Prospero's matchless words upon his lips."

There is one, and only one, exception to the "seven songless years." In 1878 Thomson wrote a poem which was, as usual, strongly biographical. Since he never finished it, he prevented it from ever being published, and the sketch has long since been destroyed. But Dobell, in his excellent Memoir prefixed to the 1895 volume of collected poems, has, despite the poet's own injunctions, quoted several striking stanzas, and given a prose summary of the rest.

In a prose postscript to this poem which Dobell reprints, Thomson remarks concerning it, "writing the foregoing lines I have felt like a man making his will at the gates of Death, summing up life's scars." We have little reason to question Dobell's assertion that Thomson here "laid bare his inmost soul." Yet he found that the poem was "too hard and harsh in both conception and execution for attempt at polishing—far more truth than poetry in it." That Dobell did not publish it complete in spite of the poet's wishes, is perhaps the only mistake he made when editing the poet's complete works.

According to his summary of the poem, Thomson attributed his life-long unhappiness to the death of Matilda. After that tragedy, his mind had fed upon itself, all Faith, Hope and Love departed from him, and only his grief remained. Although on the whole he would have preferred to die, his art as a poet consoled him to some extent. Suffering and reflection had taught him that Immortality was a delusion, and that therefore Matilda, who might have given his life happiness and success, was eternally lost to him. So greatly did he think the pains of life outweighed its joys, that even if his youth with her could be restored, he would not now selfishly accept it. She was now eternally at rest, as he too shortly expected to be. These utterly hopeless views Thomson states without artistic allegory, but tersely and with entirely frank self-analysis. The whole poem shows that these seven years of poetic apathy were quite the most painful of the poet's life, since there was no escape as before into the kindly illusion that creative poetry afforded him. This nameless poem, however faithfully it summarizes the poet's whole life, is probably a still more accurate record of his inner life during the "seven songless years."

William M. Rossetti, with whom Thomson had long corresponded, both concerning his own poems, and various aspects of Shelley's works, wrote an acute description of Thomson's appearance at this time:

"He came one evening, when the only person at home with me was my elder sister (authoress of *A Shadow of Dante*). I saw him partly alone and partly in my sister's company. Thomson was a rather small man—hardly five feet six in height—with sufficiently regular features, bright eyes, and at that time a cheerful, pleasant manner. There was (but I think only in later years) a rather peculiar expression in his mouth; something of a permanently pained expression, along with a settled half-smile, caustic but not cynical; not 'put on,' but adopted as part of his attitude toward the world. I had expected to find him rather of the type of the intellectual working-man, but did not find this to be the fact; he seemed to me more of the 'city-clerk' or minor man of business with literary tastes. His manners were good, free from nervousness, pretension or self-assertion. He talked extremely well, and without, I think, any symptom of defective education, except that his *h's* were sometimes less aspirated than they should be. Not that he *dropped his h's,* and he certainly never inserted them where they ought not to come. There was no trace of the Scotchman in his pronunciation. We passed a pleasant evening, and I can recollect that my sister, who was an intense religious devotee, received an agreeable impression from his conversation—which shows that he knew when to keep his strong opinions to himself. . . . I never saw him out of temper, vehement or noticeably gloomy; his demeanor mostly (so far as I saw it) was that of a man of habitually low spirits, who did not allow these to affect his manner in society or the tone of his conversation."

# CHAPTER VII

## LAST DAYS (1881-1882)

THOMSON was not, however, doomed to die in the apathetic state of decay which characterized the "seven songless years." Fate took care that his spirit should not be dulled into insensibility by failure. At this critical turning point in his career, destiny again endowed him with a modicum of success, that his hopes might be reinvigorated, and his final defeat rendered the more bitter. In 1880, when the poet had almost given up hope of ever printing his collected poems, Dobell succeeded in persuading Reeves & Turner to publish in book form Thomson's *City* and other chief poems. Until now, copies of the *City* were practically unobtainable, as it had been printed only in the *National Reformer,* and in sections. This 1880 volume was modestly successful, and was fairly well reviewed. The most flattering attention came from Meredith in a letter of April 27:

" . . . In writing to you about this admirable and priceless book of verse I have wished to be competent to express my feeling for your merit, and as much as possible the

[ 114 ]

praise of such rarely equalled good work. My friends could tell you that I am a critic hard to please. They say that irony lurks in my eulogy. . . . Well, I have gone through your volume, and partly a second time, and I have not found the line I would propose to recast. I have found many pages that no other English poet could have written. Nowhere is the verse feeble, nowhere is the expression insufficient; the majesty of the line has always its full coloring, and marches under a banner. And you accomplish this effect with the utmost sobriety, with absolute self-mastery."

As the result of their subsequent correspondence, Thomson made the acquaintance of Meredith, and on the 29th of June spent a day with him at Dorking. Thomson had been a reader of the "prose Browning's" novels when they were receiving very little attention from the general reading public. His diary records his pleasure at this visit:

"*July 1st*—Spent with Meredith, a real red-letter day in all respects. He is one of those personalities who need fear no comparison with their best works."

The success of the 1880 volume encouraged Thomson to turn again to the writing of poetry.

In 1881 he wrote two good poems, *A Voice from the Nile* and *Richard Forest's Midsummer Night*, beside a few trifling verses on occasional subjects. It is not without significance that of these two poems with which he broke his seven years' silence, one is joyful and the other sad. The *Midsummer Night* is a passionate lyric medley of love, which in certain parts rivals, although somewhat dangerously suggests, Tennyson's *Maud*. Nothing could seem further from the terrible visions and sounds of the *City* than these richly melodious love-songs:

"Oh, how the nights are short,
    These heavenly nights of June!
The long day all amort
With toil, the time to court
    So stinted in its boon.

"When deep in fern we lie
    With golden gorse above;
Deep sapphire sea and sky,
Ringing of larks on high
    One whole world breathing love.

"The Spring renews its youth
    And youth renews its spring;
Love's wildest dreams are truth,
Magic is sober sooth;
    Charm of the Magic Ring."

Yet only one month before, the same poet had written in *A Voice from the Nile*, of the unceas-

ing law of change in the universe, and of the
instability of all human things. The reader looks
in vain for Thomson's former fierce vividness of
phrase:

"Dusk memories haunt me of an infinite past
Ages and cycles brood above my springs,
Though I remember not my primal birth.
So ancient is my being and august,
I know not anything more venerable;
Unless, perchance, the vaulting skies that
    hold
The sun and moon and stars that shine on
    me,
The air that breathes upon me with de-
    light,
And Earth, All-Mother, all-beneficent,
Who held her mountains forth like opulent
    breasts
To cradle me and feed me with their snows,
And hollowed out the great sea to receive
My overplus of flowing energy:
Blessed for ever be our Mother Earth."

This brief monologue, the only blank verse
that Thomson ever wrote, has an intellectual calm
which is new. Its pessimism is the impersonal
intellectual pessimism of Matthew Arnold. Although mankind seems to Thomson a tragic out-
growth of blind nature, a chance product which

now at last has grown conscious of its tenuous
and hopeless position, yet for the moment he
holds himself as an artist securely aloof from the
process:

> "For thirty generations of my corn
> Outlast a generation of my men,
> And thirty generations of my men
> Outlast a generation of their gods:
> O admirable, pitiable man,
> My child yet alien in my family."

In the fall of 1880, another collection of
Thomson's poems, entitled, *Vane's Story, and
Other Poems*," had been published by Dobell
through Reeves & Turner, but did not sell well.
In 1881 a collection of Thomson's prose called
*"Essays and Phantasies"* met with an equally unfortunate and quite undeserved fate. Of this edition only three hundred copies survived a fire at
the printer's. The account which Mr. Salt gives
of these publications is rather misleading, as he
quite overestimates their success.

The winter of 1881-1882 was consequently a
rather gloomy one for the poet. A letter of
January 5, 1881, is typical:

"With Mr. Wright and Percy (Holyoake) I went to George Eliot's funeral. It
was wretched tramping through the slush,
and then standing in the rain for about three-

quarters of an hour, with nothing to see but dripping unbrellas. I was disappointed at there being any chapel service at all. At the grave old Dr. Sadler mumbled something, of which only two or three words could be distinguished by us, only a couple of yards behind him."

Shortly after the novelist's death, Thomson projected a critical study of her writings for Reeves & Turner. This work was abandoned eventually for a similar study of Heine, which in the course of time was also abandoned.

Early in March, 1881, Thomson was introduced by his friend, T. Wright, to a Mr. J. W. Barrs of Leicester. An intimate friendship between him and the poet rapidly ensued, and in June of the same year Thomson paid him a visit of over five weeks. In many poems before this, especially in *Sunday at Hampstead*, Thomson had shown the intense pleasure which he took in slight departures from the drab routine of his life as a literary hack in London. In society, the nervous reaction from the torturing cares which so often oppressed him, rendered him a lively and sprightly personality. This typical mood had made him popular with men and women all his life. During this particular visit in 1881, he seems from his letters for a time quite to have thrown off the deadening personal despair with which his mechanical duties in fog-ridden London usually enshrouded him. Both the *Voice from the Nile* and the *Midsummer Night* were conceived and executed here. Of this pleasant visit Thomson wrote Dobell:

"We are here four miles from Leicester, with railroad station a few minutes off, in a pleasant villa, surrounded by shrubbery, lawn, meadow, and kitchen garden. Host and hostess (sister) are kindness itself, as are all other Leicester friends. We lead the most healthy of lives, save to strong temptations to over-feeding on excellent fare, and host's evil and powerfully contagious habit of sitting up till about 2 A. M. smoking and reading or chatting. I now leave him to his own wicked devices at midnight, or as soon after as possible. Despite showery weather we have had good drives and walks (country all green and well-wooded), jolly little picnics and lawn tennis ad infinitum (N. B. Lawn tennis even more than lady's fine pen responsible for the uncouthness of this scrawl.) In brief, we have been so busy with enjoyment that this is the first note I have accomplished (or begun) in seventeen days."

From the Barrs' home Thomson accompanied Wright on a business trip before returning to

London. His copious correspondence with the
Barrs family dates from a letter of June 25 to
Miss Barrs:

"Raining hard since 6 in the morning (not
that I was up to see it begin). . . . General
despair as to hay unmown, or mown and
lying unstacked. Special despair of B. V.
(Beautiful Virtue, mind!) who has to
scrawl instead of rambling. . . .

"Phil Wright having all his things in the
other sleeping chamber, I have the honour
of sleeping in the wonderful bedstead which
Mr. and Mrs. Noah used in the ark some
short time ago. Under the beneficent pro-
tection of the good angel with the scanty
wings & the ample nose, and sustained by a
flawless conscience, I slept the sleep of the
just. . . .

"I must not inflict any more of my pluvial
*ennui* upon you just now, as I am about writing for the first time to my good landlady,
who is a credit to her sex, and who may be
getting anxious about her model lodger."

From these letters one would never think of
Thomson as the author of the terrible *City*. As
we have seen, this idyllic vacation together with
the measured success of Dobell's attempts at pub-
lishing his works, particularly the first volume of
1880, had broken the apathetic spell which had

hung over the poet during the "seven songless
years." Even by January he had not forgotten
his visit to Leicester, as we see by his tender and
cheerful stanzas *At Belvoir:*

"My thoughts go back to last July,
    Sweet happy thoughts and tender;
'The bridal of the earth and sky,'
    A day of noble splendor;
A day to make the saddest heart
    In joy a true believer;
When two good friends we roamed apart
    The shady walks of Belvoir.

"Yet, now and then a quiet word
    Of seriousness dissembling
In smiles would touch some hidden chord
    And set it all a-trembling:
I trembled too, and felt it strange—
    Could I be in possession
Of music richer in its range
    Than yet had found expression?

"My thoughts go on to next July,
    More happy thoughts, more tender;
'The bridal of the earth and sky,'
    A day of perfect splendor;
A day to make the saddest heart
    In bliss a firm believer;
When two True Loves may roam apart
    The shadiest walks of Belvoir."

This poem, quoted so extensively more from its personal than its artistic interest, bore the sub-title, "A ballad, historical and prophetic." Beneath its easy good nature, one can see the poet conscious of new and mellower poetic powers, as he transports himself out of dreary London in midwinter to this eagerly anticipated season of delightful leisure in July, 1882. What results these new poetic powers, whose presence he felt within him, would have produced, no one can ever tell, except from one later poem, *He Heard Her Sing*. Fate stood also in the path of his prophesied visit, for by July, 1882, he had been dead for a month.

The story of the last five months of Thomson's life is a painful chronicle of the rapid decay of a noble nature. His old despair again made his days hopeless, and his nights a sleepless and intolerable burden. His fits of intemperance came more frequently and scourged him more terribly than ever before. Flaws, who knew him intimately during the tragic spring of 1882, has vividly described his appearance, which the portrait of Mr. Salt's biography, taken this year, fully corroborates:

"He looked like a veteran scarred in fierce affrays of life's war, and worn by the strain of forced marches. . . . you could see the shadow 'tremendous fate' had cast over that

[ 123 ]

naturally buoyant nature. It had eaten great furrows into his broad brow, and cut tear-tracks downwards from his wistful eyes, so plaintive and brimful of unspeakable tenderness as they opened wide when in serious talk."

The curse of melancholia, which his mother had bestowed upon him, had wrecked his life, and now his father's fatal weakness of intemperance was also come upon him, to drive him to his death, despairingly at first, and then with a torpid indifference still more terrible. Fate had vouchsafed him but one singing year, after the seven that were songless. Whether or not, had he lived, he could have written poetry worthy of his ironically confident note in *Belvoir*—and both Bertram Dobell and George Meredith asserted that he could in no uncertain terms—it was not destined to be.

During the first month of 1882, Thomson seems hardly to have had any inkling of his tragic death so close at hand. Besides *Belvoir* he wrote two other poems, *The Sleeper* and *Proem,* whose quiet and melodious melancholy resembles the Pre-Raphaelites. In the first poem he contemplates the slumbers of a young and beautiful girl, still pathetically his lost love, though now a dimmer and more artistically conventionalized figure than in his burning memories in *Vane's Story* or the *Fadeless Bower*. He is led to contrast her peaceful dream and his own painful waking reality. Unlike the terrible dead beauty in the *City,* drawn with fiery and almost Dantean strokes, this slumberer is described with a calm and gentle resignation. The *Proem* on the other hand looks wistfully backward upon the "antique fables, beautiful and bright" in which the happy pagan ages trusted. Since that time the world had grown old and self-conscious, and its cares had become oppressive. Immortality seemed half a phantasy, and only Love remained as man's refuge from Fate. The poem reminds one of the *Prologue to the Earthly Paradise,* except that Thomson had lived more bitterly, thought more deeply and dreamed less colorfully than Morris.

During the next month of February, Thomson wrote for the last time a poem which possesses his former rapture, and recalls Matilda, dead now for almost thirty years. Few of his poems have such sensuously beautiful detail, such liquid melody, or are impelled by such glowing confidence in Love's triumph over the indifference of Fate. Here Nature itself has felt the reviving touch of Spring:

> "We were now in the midmost Maytime, in
>     the full green flood of the Spring,
> When the air is sweet all the daytime with
>     the blossoms and birds that sing;

When the air is rich all the night, and richest of all in its noon
When the nightingales pant the delight and
keen stress of their love to the moon;
When the almond and apple and pear
spread wavering wavelets of snow
In the light of the soft warm air far-flushed
with a delicate glow;
When the towering chestnuts uphold their
masses of spires red and white,
And the pendulous tresses of gold of the
slim laburnum burn bright,
And the lilac guardeth the bowers with the
gleam of a lifted spear,
And the scent of the hawthorn flowers
breathes all the new life of the year
     \*     \*     \*     \*     \*

"And the flowers are everywhere budding
and blowing about our feet,
The green of the meadows star-studding
and the bright green blades of the
wheat."

Through the whole poem, which in meter if not
in spirit is reminiscent of Swinburne's *Hymn to
Proserpina,* there recurs the confident refrain:

"Love, love only, for ever, love with its
torture of bliss
All the world's glories can never equal two
souls in one kiss."

Apparently the new powers, whose first flush he had apprehended in *Belvoir,* were about to become articulate, and to utter with an unaccustomed joy the love that had only tormented him. Yet in the same month Thomson, in a very intimate and melancholy confession of his artistic powers, wrote *The Poet and the Muse.* Here he feels that, however joyous the past poetry of his youth had been, now it had grown gloomy and bitter. He realizes that his art is his only refuge from life, now that Love is dead. Yet he feels that even these poetic powers of his are slipping from his control. At the end he summons courage, however, and declares that if only because he could suffer bitterly, his artistic faculties were still his own:

"I am half torpid yet I spurn this lore,
   I am long silent yet cannot avow
My singing voice is lost for evermore;
    For lo, this beating heart, this burning
      brow,
This spirit gasping in keen spasms of dread
And fierce revulsion that it is not dead,
   This agony of the sting:
What soulless clod would have these tears
    and sobbings,
These terrors that are hopes, these passion-
    ate throbbings?

Dear Muse, revive! we yet may dream and
   love and sing!"

Apart from the obvious sincerity of *The Poet
and the Muse,* it might perhaps be dismissed as
a melancholy but frequent mood of the poet, were
it not for the illustration he gave of his failing
powers during the next month. Only three poems
survive from March, 1882, and two of them,
*Law vs. Gospel* and *A Stranger,* clearly show a
lesser intellectual grasp of, and a fading emotional interest in, life. The *Stranger* is a rather
tediously melancholy *terza rima* poem written
with the pathetic gentleness of a once powerful
mind, weakened by the ceaseless onslaughts of
Fate. *Law vs. Gospel* is a mediocre and hastily
written *jeu d'esprit,* which alludes sarcastically to
Bradlaugh and censures the intolerance of moral
reformers. Thomson was sinking again into a
songless year, apathetically and inevitably. But
just as the terrible *City* was the precursor to the
seven songless years of 1874-1881, so in *Insomnia,* written this March and before the period
which was destined to be songless because the
singer was dying, Thomson burned out the last
of his poetic energies forever in the most terrible
poem of his whole career. In the sombre and
awful imagery of which he was so powerful and
unique a master, he describes his interminable
nights of waking despair:

"I let my lids fall, sick of thought and sense,
    But felt that Shadow heavy on my heart;
And saw the night before me an immense
    Black waste of ridge-walls, hour by hour
        apart,
Dividing deep ravines: from ridge to ridge
Sleep's flying hour was an aerial bridge;
    But I, whose hours stood fast,
Must climb down painfully each steep side
        hither,
And climb more painfully each steep side
        thither,
And so make one hour's span for years of
        travail last.

"Thus I went down into that first ravine,
    Wearily, slowly, blindly and alone,
Staggering, stumbling, sinking depths un-
        seen,
Shaken and bruised and gashed by stub and
        stone;
And at the bottom paven with slipperiness,
A torrent-brook rushed headlong with such
        stress
    Against my feeble limbs,
Such fury of wave and foam and icy bleak-
        ness
Buffeting insupportably my weakness
That when I would recall dazed memory
        swirls and swims.

"How I got through I know not, faint as
    death;
  And then I had to climb the awful scarp,
Creeping with many a pause for panting
    breath,
    Clinging to tangled root and rock-jut
    sharp;
Perspiring with faint chills instead of heat,
Trembling, and bleeding hands and knees
    and feet;
    Falling, to rise anew;
Until, with lamentable toil and travel
Upon the ridge of arid sand and gravel
I lay supine half-dead and heard the bells
    chime Two."

There is none of his frequent joy in color and
beauty, no saving memory of his lost love, nor
any melody of words in this last terrible poem.
The words compose a harsh music which was real
to him then, although as he well knew, ugly and
dark:

"I look back on the words already written,
  And writhe by cold rage stung, by self-scorn
    smitten,
  They are so weak and vain and infinitely
    inane. . . . "

Thomson's sincere pleasure in his art had
really done very much in keeping him alive ever

since the death of Matilda in 1853. Now he knew that his art had also been denied him, and that the end was therefore not far off. The struggle with his melancholia, darkening as the years went by, and his sensitive eye and heart, which caused him to see beauty and love in the world, were now done, and melancholy had finally triumphed. His cheerfulness, which survived even the *City*, his memory of Matilda which only a month past he had been again contemplating with a warm joyousness, and his hopes of yet writing happier and nobler poems—all these were at last laid aside for ever. Of his poetical career, the rest was silence.

It is both painful and unnecessary to dwell on the last two months of Thomson's life. He lived through them quite alone, the unresisting victim of alcohol and insomnia. His old courage was so completely gone that he seems to have been indifferent to his fast approaching doom. Only two occasional verses survive from these months, both poorly written bits of hackwork. *The Old Story and the New Storey,* written in April, is an attack upon the English humanitarians who were objecting to the unfair cost of monarchical upkeep; *Despotism tempered by Dynamite,* written in May, is a bitter attack upon the hateful tyranny of the White Tsar. The latter is the last poem Thomson ever wrote.

Of the very last of the poet's life, all his biog-

raphers present a similar but vague account.
G. G. Flaws wrote:

"Let it not be misread as a harshness, or
as a lightly tripped-off phrase, when I give
out that, in all verity to me, his later life was
a slow suicide, perceived and acquiesced in
deliberately by himself.

"Even his friends in Gower Street lost
control of him, and did not know his whereabouts. Thomson was so reckless, because
his visit to Leicester had ended in a fit of
intemperance, and he returned to London in
bitter remorse and despair. Percy Holyoake
was looking everywhere for him on June 1st,
when he visited Marston for the last time."

Bertram Dobell has added:

"He eagerly anticipated the time when it
(drink) should destroy him. . . . How he
lived during the last three or four weeks of
his existence can only be conjectured, for he
had now no longer a regular home, but slept
in common lodging-houses. Sometimes, it
is to be feared, he was numbered amongst the
homeless and shelterless wanderers of the
streets."

The merciless City had at last claimed its victim.
William Sharp has described his last hours:

"For a few weeks his record is almost a blank. When the direst straits were reached, he so reconquered his control that he felt himself able to visit one whose sympathy and regard had withstood all tests. Thomson found Philip Marston alone; the latter soon realized that his friend was mentally distraught, and endured a harrowing experience, into the narration of which I do not care to enter.

"I arrived in the late afternoon and found Marston in a state of nervous perturbation. Thomson was lying down on the bed in the adjoining room: stooping, I caught his whispered words that he was dying; upon that I lit a match, and in the sudden glare beheld his white face on the blood-stained pillow. He had burst one or more blood-vessels, and the haemorrhage was dreadful.

"Some time had to elapse before anything could be done, but ultimately with the aid of a friend who came in opportunely, poor Thomson was carried downstairs, and having been placed in a cab, was driven to the adjoining University Hospital."

The next day Sharp with the blind poet, Marston, visited Thomson there. The last recorded appearance of Thomson alive has again been preserved by Sharp:

[ 133 ]

"Nor can I ever forget the look of profound despair in the eyes of the dying man in the ward at the University College Hospital—the despair of what De Quincey has called a 'blazing misery,' though without relation to any future of possible weal or woe."

Salt speaks vaguely but kindly of the poet's dying words, while Sharp, who probably heard them, hints with painful truth that they were dreadful to hear. No one has preserved them. Thomson died in the evening of June 3, 1882, two days after the fatal attack in Marston's chambers. Five days afterwards he was buried in the Highgate Cemetery, in the same grave where, eight years before, his friend Austin Holyoake had been laid to rest. Only a few of his most intimate friends, such as his younger brother, John Thomson, T. R. Wright, Percy Holyoake, J. W. Barrs, Miss Barrs and Marston, were present. With Thomson was interred a locket containing a tress of yellow hair, his one memento of his lost love. Out of respect to the dead man's heterodox views, there was no religious service. Salt has preserved the burial service which was adapted for the occasion by Percy Holyoake, and also the "elegant and feeling tribute to the virtues of the man and the genius of the poet" which was delivered by Holyoake at the grave. At last the

wistful invocation, which over twenty years before
the poet had made in *Our Ladies of Death,* had
been fulfilled for him:

> "Take me and lull me into perfect sleep;
>     Down, down, far hidden in thy duskiest
>         cave;
> While all the clamorous years above me
>         sweep
>     Unheard, or, like the voice of seas that
>         rave
> On far-off coasts, but murmuring o'er my
>         trance,
> A dim, vast monotone, that shall enhance
>     The restful rapture of the inviolate
>         grave."

This is the end of Thomson the man; the end
of Thomson the poet is not yet.

# CHAPTER VIII

## CRITICISM

THE defense of a poet is usually poor enough criticism, for the writer must at once plunge into the dust and heat of partizanship. It is very difficult for the advocate to weigh evidence rather than shape it to his purpose. Yet in the case of Thomson, any fair and intelligent criticism must necessarily be a defense, for the poet's name and works survive chiefly as horrible hearsay phantoms. Men who have never read a word of his poetry or his prose gain somehow, year after year, the general impression that Thomson was an immoral and blasphemous man who wrote, some years since, several very pessimistic poems in a rough, harsh style that quite lacks distinction. Be it our task to inquire into the more significant phases of this wan, hearsay reputation which the poet at present possesses, that we may do even a scant justice to one of the most original, powerful and sincere poets of the last century.

Something has already been said of the melancholy life of Thomson, and his lingering death from drink in 1882. As a concession to the habitually moral critic of poets and poetry, mention might be made of Coleridge, Chatterton, Byron, Poe, De Quincey, Rossetti, Swinburne, and perhaps Keats, as artists whose lives were not clear from an even fatal indulgence in stimulants. Yet Thomson lived for the most part within his own mind, and such external criticism fails to arrive at the heart of the man. Like Coleridge, Thomson became fatally absorbed in himself, and from brooding upon his own irresolute powers of mind, became a pessimist. Coleridge in his *Ode on Dejection* had written:

> "O Lady! We receive but what we give,
>   And in our life alone does Nature live:
>   Ours is her wedding-garment, ours her
>       shroud!
>   And would we aught behold, of higher
>       worth,
> Than that inanimate cold world allowed
> To the poor loveless ever-anxious crowd,
>   Ah! from the soul itself must issue forth
> A light, a glory, a fair luminous cloud
>   Enveloping the Earth—
> And from the soul itself there must be sent
>   A sweet and potent voice, of its own birth,
> Of all sweet sounds the life and element!"

Thomson came to know the truth of this poem only too well. Yet his brooding melancholy was largely inherent in his nature from his earliest days. Novalis has somewhere said that "Character is Fate," and in Thomson's case the epigram is tragically true. His love died early in his career, his youthful religious beliefs were so rigid that they could not survive the inevitable doubtings of maturity, a life of action was prevented by his literary tendencies, his literary labors went almost without notice or approval most of his life, and he could not identify himself with Nature because of his self-awareness and his city life. Thomson was thus unable to sink himself into any external interest, and so save himself from his terrible self-analysis. Under immediate stimulus, his talk and his letters were almost invariably cheerful, but when leisure allowed him to ponder, his poems were usually dark and sorrowful.

Yet this fatalism of his is not at all ignoble. It should be pitied, not reprehended. Thomson believed when his despairing mood was upon him, that

> "I find no hint throughout the Universe
>   Of good or ill, of blessing or of curse;
>   I find alone Necessity supreme."

Yet until the last two months of his life, he fought bitterly against the inevitable. Except perhaps in the *Lord of the Castle of Indolence,* his poetry shows no signs of the Oriental submission to Fate.

Certainly the generation which reads the Rubaiyat of Fitzgerald with relish, can scarcely afford to censure the heroic struggle with Destiny which Thomson maintains in the conclusion to the *City*. Like the greatest writers of his race, from the unknown author of the Beowulf to Thomas Hardy, he never ceased to oppose Fate with all the power that was in him, and the passionate intensity of *Mater Tenebrarum,* the *Ladies of Death,* or the *City* is a tribute to a mighty courage. Since he would not bend, he broke at the last.

Much also has been made of his occasional cynicism, as in *Art* or *Vane's Story*. These cynical passages, however, represent merely the comparatively infrequent moments when he found himself too worn out with the sad difference between the ideal and the actual world, to blaze with his usual fiery indignation at the tragic disparity. Although he lacked any sort of formal religious faith, few poets have loved the truth as much, or sought for it as eagerly. Those who have called his clinging to his dead love an immoral weakness need to be reminded of Dante, Novalis, and the Philistine's habit of "marrying his deceased wife's sister."

As to Thomson's blasphemy, much understanding is again needed. Sincere blasphemy of the kind which he occasionally wrote, as in *Vane's Story* or *Bill Jones on Prayer,* is, paradoxically enough, the sign of a profoundly religious nature. There is no casual impudence about it. The poet had been unable to escape his early upbringing in an atmosphere of original sin, total depravity, and all the other morbid horrors of Calvinism against which Burns and Carlyle have spoken with no uncertain tone. It is not for most of us, who smile at Mid-Victorian theology, to criticise Thomson for nobler, wiser and more acute criticisms of it than our own. Actually, Thomson was never an unreligious man, nor could he for long escape spiritual problems. His blasphemies were caused by the failure of the actual church which he saw to correspond to the lofty ideal which his poetic idealism had created for it.

Many critics have objected to the rough, harsh style of his poetry, and this objection cannot be dismissed so lightly. Even William Sharp's charge of "rhetorical verbiage, and a vulgar recklessness of expression" is not without foundation. The poet's use of archaic and original words, of double words, of monotonous epithets and imperfect rhymes, is indeed too pronounced, even in his mature work. Thomson was for the most part self-educated in literature, and his sense of poetic form was sometimes more mathematical than artistic. There are occasional touches like those of "Johnny Keats," except that Thomson sins in clumsy over-seriousness rather than mawkish prettiness. Certain phases of the crudely powerful and earnest style of Thomson's poetry, remind one of Carlyle's prose. Yet this charge of harsh diction, true as it is, can be pressed too far. In a private conversation, Alfred Noyes once remarked to me that Thomson was too rough and lacked art. Afterwards, as is usually the case, I thought of the reply I should have made at the time. According to the old Greek myth, out of Chaos came order, and out of order came the Muses. In plain language, poetry organizes the world in order to extract meaning out of it. The poet's world is usually consistent because it has been well ordered. Just as his world is more regular and patterned than the real world, so his language is more regular and more patterned than the ordinary unmetrical language of prose or speech. Tennyson's line is smooth because it is expressing a world which he has smoothed out beforehand. Hence it comes that readers expect the poet to organize a meaning out of the world, and consequently write rather smooth verses about it. But Thomson differs from most poets in that very often he is attempting to express Chaos, and not an ordered universe at all. What he was trying to express was not the harmony of life, but the meaningless discords of it, and to do this successfully uncouthness is absolutely necessary. So Lucretius had found it in *"De Rerum Natura,"* so did that master of poetic technique, Milton, find it in the *Paradise Lost* when he wrote of

"Rocks, caves, lakes, fens, bogs, dens, and
    shades of death—"

Had Thomson forgotten the truth of what he was
writing for the mere beauty of insincere expression, such a rough stanza as

"The world rolls round for ever like a mill;
  It grinds out death and life and good and
    ill;
  It has no purpose, heart or mind or will"

would lack its powerful sincerity. Consequently,
his rough lines are very often not only justifiable
but felicitous in expressing what he was attempting to express. Despite Tennyson and the school
of Tennyson, poetry cannot be measured only by
its smoothness. Browning's assertion of much the
same principle finds more consent now than it did
when Tennyson's influence on English poetry was
supreme. Thomson satirized this insincere over-
smoothness in his *Real Vision of Sin,* and was
usually far too much in earnest to disguise his real
meaning with a bland beauty of utterance. In this
respect, it is natural though unfortunate that he
should have the defects of his qualities.

Thomson has also been severely criticised for
his receptivity. Critics have pointed out in his
poems the strong and successive influence of Shelley, Browning, Leopardi, Arnold, Dante, Heine,

Swinburne, Rossetti, and even Tennyson, especially in the poems written before 1862, and during the period when his powers were maturing. Yet such imitation is indeed the general rule among young poets. But as he grew older, his prolix flow of rich and original metaphors was curbed, and his best poems are in a stern and inevitably powerful style. In such spirit, at least, *In the Room*, the *City, Weddah, The fire that filled my heart of old* and *Insomnia* were composed. Certainly no other poet in English literature could well have written these poems. At his best Thomson possesses an almost unique balance between his relentless logical faculties and his intense and sweeping imagination. Shelley was too imaginative and Browning too intellectual to attain such Dantean power as the best passages of the *City* reveal. In fact, the resemblance between Thomson and the Florentine is not as superficial as on first sight it might seem. Both poets' loves died young, to both the universe seemed stern and predetermined. The fact that one took a single City to embody human life, while the other found it necessary to employ the whole known universe, is after all a difference in degree rather than kind. Thomson once called Dante "the central intellect of the world," and consciously imitated his style. In Thomson's several experiments with *terza rima,* and in his frequent allusions to the great Italian, the younger poet shows the results of constant and intense reading of the *Divina Commedia*.

But the chief and perhaps least valid of the stock objections to Thomson's poetry is its pessimism. That all great poets have a streak of this in their natures, is obvious. That Thomson's peculiar pessimism is neither ignoble nor his only attitude toward life, has been sufficiently illustrated. The question, therefore, which the critic of poetry must ask himself, is whether he has expressed this feeling fully, sincerely and powerfully, and few who read Thomson's best poems can deny that he has done this.

In the Proem to the *City,* as well as in many other poems, Thomson declared that he well knew that his poetry was not a true expression of the lives of everyone. He did not wish, as Swift had, to kill the whole human race, and he declined upon reflection to kill himself. He bore the habitual optimist no envy, but much of his best poetry he addressed to the "sad confraternity" who like himself wandered hopelessly in the "dolent city." He is not therefore insanely unbalanced at all, nor does he exaggerate. Dante could never have written the *Inferno* had he not also been capable of writing the *Paradiso.* Thomson's gloom is intense because he could also rejoice greatly. As a matter of fact, very few of the critics who shake their heads in disapproval over his pessimism, ever felt half the beauty or the joy which Thomson has put into *Sunday up the River*. According to these men, Thomson must be a formula, an unswerving type of something or other. They cannot seem to see that he was a man, self-contradictory as any living man always is, constantly wavering between joy and despair, a love of beauty and a hatred of life, a passionate yearning for his dead love and a stern desire for oblivion. Thomson expressed these things because he was a poet, and his expression of them is intense because he was a genius. His pessimism, when it was upon him, was the sincere conviction of a man of industry, high ideals, strong will, sound brain and great poetical ability. It cannot be lightly set aside by men who dare no irreverence to the heath scenes in *Lear,* or the Malebolge in the *Inferno*.

It is one of the perennial tragedies of literature that Fate sows poets frequently on barren ground. What Thomson might have accomplished under happier circumstances has been ably conjectured by George Meredith, the greatest critic of Thomson's acquaintance:

"I had full admiration of his nature and his powers. Few men have been endowed with so brave a heart. He did me the honour to visit me twice, when I was unaware of the tragic affliction overclouding him, but I could see that he was badly weighed. I have now the conviction that the taking away of poverty from his burdens would in all likelihood have saved him, to enrich our literature; for his verse was a pure well. He had, almost past example in my experience, the thrill of the worship of moral valiancy as well as of sensuous beauty; his narrative poem *Weddah and Om-el-Bonain* stands to witness what great things he would have done in the exhibition of nobility at war with evil conditions.

"He probably had, as most of us have had, his heavy suffering on the soft side. But he inherited the tendency to the thing that slew him, and it is my opinion that, in consideration of his high and singularly elective mind, he might have worked clear of it to throw it off, if circumstances had been smoother and brighter about him. For thus he would have been saved from drudgery, had time to labor at the conceptions that needed time for the maturing and definition even before the evolvement of them. He would have had what was also much needed in his case, a more spacious home, a more companioned life, more than visiting friends, good and true to him though they were. A domestic centre of any gracious kind would have sheathed his over-active, sensational imaginativeness, to give it rest, and enabled him to feel the delight of drawing it forth bright and keen of edge."

Life itself is a dazzling and bewildering whirl of colors, and each artist who would paint it, must pick from it what hues he will. Some will paint it in azures, crimsons, and rich purple and gold, others in dingy drabs and greys. In so far only as he is sincere and gets a meaning out of its iridescent complexity, is he an artist. And this also Thomson knew, for he has written in his introductory note to the *Lady of Sorrows:*

"That this composition is true in relation to the author, that it is genuine, I have no doubt, for the poor fellow had large gifts for being unhappy. But is it true in relation to the world and general life? I think true, but not the whole truth. There is the truth of winter and black night, there is the truth of summer and dazzling noonday; on the one side of the great medal are stamped the glory and the triumph of life, on the other side are stamped the glory and the triumph of death; but which is the obverse and which the reverse none of us surely knows."

Pessimism may prevent Thomson from ever being popular, as it has Leopardi and, despite conventional sentiment to the contrary, Dante himself.  Yet at least his poetry must always be respected by the "judicious reader," as it will always be understood and appreciated by such as themselves have "paced that dolent city," overcome by the "melancholia that transcends all wit."

FINIS

*On train in Ohio*
*10 March 1917*